SUFFER THE CHILDREN

SUFFER
THE
CHILDREN

A Pediatrician's Reflections on Abuse

Rosamond L. Murdock, M.D.

Foreword by Mariette Hartley

HEALTHPRESS
P.O. DRAWER 1388
SANTA FE, NM 87504

Published by Health Press
PO Drawer 1388
Santa Fe, NM 87504

96 95 94 93 92   5 4 3 2 1

Library of Congress Cataloging-in-Publication Data

   Murdock, Rosamond L., 1931–
            Suffer the Children : A Pediatrician's Reflections on Abuse /
   Rosamond L. Murdock ; foreword by Mariette Hartley
        p.   cm.
   Includes bibliographical references and index.
   ISBN 0-929173-09-0

     1. Child abuse. 2. Child abuse—Government policy—United States.
I. Title.
   [DNLM: 1. Child Abuse.   WA 320 M974s]
RC569.5.C55M87 1992
616.85'822—dc20
DNLM/DLC
for Library of Congress   91-35371
                                                CIP

Cover design and illustration by Paulette Livers Lambert
Text graphics by Ida A. Marx
Edited by Susan Victor

TABLE OF CONTENTS

FOREWORD

One child, abandoned, abused or sexually molested, is one too many. It is time that we as a society not only look at the abuse that goes on behind closed doors but also become responsible for it.

A family should be a safe place, a place where early nurturing and warmth create responsive, empathetic, loving children and future adults. The sad fact is that many children do not have to leave their homes to be raped or beaten—it is being perpetrated upon them by the very people who "raise" them.

Who is culpable here? How do courts handle these miscarriages of justice? Is it indeed more dangerous for some children litigate because of the terror of going into a strange and often hostile foster home? Is it also more dangerous, because reprisal at home becomes an even more unbearable hell, if the problem is made public?

A beautiful young woman with whom I've become close was such a child. She admitted to me rather guiltily one day that her father had broken thirteen bones in her body by the time she was seventeen. There was no foster home to go to, and when a well-meaning teacher confronted the parents, this child was brutally punished. She had no recourse. Unfortunately, those who try to intervene are damned if they don't succeed—and the child victim is damned if he or she speaks out.

Juanita, a bright, sensitive fourteen-year-old, chose to stay in an incestuous relationship with her father for seven years, rather than go to an unknown place. Her father committed suicide only last summer after she had suffered an abortion. She said to me recently, "I realize I probably had friends. I just didn't know it at the time."

The prevalence of child abuse in this country is overwhelming, and what I have come to be aware of as I work and meet with survivors across the country is that the injured child stays injured and becomes a dysfunctional adult. If adults tend to their inner injured child, they can become loving and viable members of society. Often the pain is great and the fear and shame attendant to the pain make their lives unbearable. Suicide then appears to be the "only answer." How many valuable, resourceful adults are we losing to childhood trauma? Far too many. Dr. Rosamond L. Murdock agrees. She gives us clarity in her frank, often brutally honest, always impressive book, *SUFFER THE CHILDREN: A Pediatrician's Reflections on Abuse.*

The need for education is great. Alice Miller, in her brilliant, pioneering work, *Drama of the Gifted Child*, set the stage, but so much more education is needed. Child abuse is rampant and in my opinion, epidemic; it must be stopped. This enlightening and loving book sheds light on all aspects of abuse. It goes into important psychological detail and case histories—situations are not judged but are explored and reported. Legacies, after all, get passed down, but legacies can and must be changed. This book is an important step in that direction. It must be read by people who care about children—and, even more importantly, by people who *don't*.

—Mariette Hartley

Emmy-award winning actress Mariette Hartley is a thirty-year veteran of television, films and theater. Her autobiography, BREAKING THE SILENCE (G.P. Putnam's Sons 1990; Signet 1991), reveals a troubled upbringing which exposed her to family alcoholism, abuse and suicide, and her physical and emotional triumph over this devastating heritage.

In addition to her busy acting career, Ms. Hartley devotes time to several social service organizations, including MADD (Mothers Against Drunk Driving), and is an honorary director of the American Suicide Foundation. She is currently involved with The Aviva Center in Los Angeles, a home for abused and runaway teenage girls, and is also active in handgun control.

ACKNOWLEDGMENTS

My sincerest "thank yous" for helping me in one way or another write this book go to the following individuals:

Dr. Andrew and Dee Mason, dear friends and neighbors, for their emotional support and guidance in writing;

Joanne Johnston, precious sister and longtime junior high school English and social studies teacher in California, for her encouragement, perspective, and resource materials; and

Attorney Nancy K. Murdock of New Hampshire, friend and confidante for thirty years, for her professional experience in child abuse cases, legal viewpoints, and much more.

INTRODUCTION

As a result of the United Nations (UN) Summit Meeting on Children in late September 1990, convening the world leaders of seventy countries, the "rights of the child" to improved health was prioritized on the international agenda. The globally mandated goal is to reduce infant and maternal mortality and child malnutrition by up to 50 percent by the year 2000, heralding a "decade of the child." Human rights and freedom movements have dramatically emerged all over the world in an attempt to overcome abusive and restrictive dictatorial regimes. The power-greedy oppressors are being thrown out by the suppressed masses. The future of these previously oppressed peoples looks brighter and the threat of global war has been substantially reduced, but for children in the United States, where child abuse and neglect has been escalating, the prospect is not so bright. Our future generations are being wasted by drugs, violence, AIDS and all forms of child abuse and neglect. During the past thirty years, our society has seen the mushrooming of self-destructive behavior by adults and children alike; the decay of morality at all levels of society; a decline in self-discipline; and the glorification of materialistic greed, which characterizes the "me" generation. Individual freedoms and opportunities have peaked, but personal responsibilities that must accompany rights and privileges are sadly lacking.

Among all the travesties of justice and of "man's inhumanity to man" that concern me, I chose to write about child abuse and neglect because it is a preventable activity, one with a profound impact on families, victims, abusers, and, ultimately, the generations to come. The abused become, in adulthood, the abusers. I would like to believe that children have the human right to "life, liberty and the pursuit of happiness" as a result of parental nurturing, protection and education. Many children are denied these rights because of poverty or ignorance but others are denied because of deliberate abuse and neglect. *It is to all children who should be allowed to grow up unscarred so they can reach their full potential that I devote this book.*

The well-being of children has been a lifelong commitment for me: first, as a mother of three children and now as a grandmother; second, as a pediatrician in private practice and public health preventive medicine clinics; third, as an administrator (State Director of School Health Services) and consultant to Maternal and Child Health and to the Handicapped Children's Program; and fourth, as an educator on the clinical teaching faculty of two medical schools. Basic to every endeavor was an emphasis on teaching child health, development, and preventive practices to parents, professionals and the public in general. I am a firm believer that education is a prime tool in preventive medicine and safety. It was during the course of my various professional experiences that I came to appreciate the long-term effects of child abuse and neglect on children who were born both physically and mentally healthy, yet who grew up scarred by abuse and neglect. The popular consensus that children born into poverty and ignorance are generally abused and neglected is not necessarily true. Parental figures who are loving, nurturing and sacrificing for their children promote the health and well-being of young people despite environmental circumstances. The unwanted child born to immature and self-centered parents is much more likely to be abused and neglected.

Child abuse and neglect is ubiquitous in that it crosses all socioeconomic, cultural, religious, geographical and educational boundaries. It is to illustrate the occurrence of child abuse/neglect in all classes of people that I have selected firsthand case histories of child victims from educated families who are not affected by poverty. Each case has been chosen as a prototype of hundreds, perhaps thousands, of like situations.

The subject of child abuse/neglect is both timeless and timely—timely because of the recent nationwide media coverage of child abuse that the general public has reacted to with repugnance and horror. Such aroused public interest should be kept in the forefront in order to prevent and combat the problem. Despite the increase in laws against it and governmental and private agencies and self-help groups to deter, prevent, treat or deal with abuse toward children, the rate of abuse has risen markedly during the past ten years. In Massachusetts alone during 1990, the rate of child abuse and neglect jumped 17 percent over the preceding year, amounting to 82,831 reported cases. The National Center for Child Abuse and Neglect in Washington, DC, recorded a nationwide rate increase of 21.7 percent for 1989. Reported cases reflect only the tip of the iceberg.

Child abuse and neglect is also timeless. Throughout the recorded history of mankind, children were abused, murdered in sacrificial rituals, starved, neglected, enslaved and sold as chattel. Today, in this century of outstanding advances, some children are undergoing the same types of suffering.

The time range of vulnerability for child abuse/neglect is vast, beginning prenatally and continuing until the age of emancipation. For females, it may continue throughout life in the forms of wife beating and later as geriatric abuse and neglect. Prenatal abuse occurs when a mother drinks alcohol, takes illegal and even legal drugs, voluntarily or involuntarily deprives her unborn of adequate nutrition, or fails to protect herself and the fetus against infectious diseases, such as rubella, herpes and AIDS.

The US Department of Health and Human Services, under which the Child Abuse Prevention and Treatment Act (1974) and Amendments (1978) were legislated, has recognized and defined several distinct forms of child abuse and neglect: physical abuse, physical neglect, sexual abuse, emotional abuse and educational neglect. Such categorical forms are for descriptive reporting purposes and are rather arbitrary since, in reality, maltreatments tend to coexist: physical and sexual abuse, sexual and emotional abuse, and any other number of combinations. I have attempted to provide an overview of each form of abuse and neglect, chapter by chapter. Pervasive to each form of maltreatment is psychological abuse. Thus, although not reported as the most prevalent abuse, it is omnipresent. The aftereffects of most types of abuse program the victims' lives: the physically abused child learns that violent behavior is the way to vent frustration and control others and may become an abusive adult. The sexually abused child may later become a prostitute, a rapist, a frigid person or a predator of children. A sense of low self-esteem is common to nearly all abused or neglected children.

Because children with curable illness have needlessly died from lack of conventional medical attention due to their parents' religious faith forbidding medical care, I have included a chapter on medical neglect. (The Child Abuse Prevention and Treatment Act, amended in 1978, states that failure to obtain medical care for a minor child is a form of neglect.)

Another troubling issue that I felt was important to address is that of youth runaways and suicides. The problem has surfaced at alarming rates in recent years. Some children are so unhappy with an event in their lives, or with their lives in general, that they must escape in desperation. Others find the only way out of utter despair is in death. The factors leading up to running away or self-destruction are often based in child abuse and neglect—the child who is repeatedly beaten or raped, the child who is made to feel unwanted and worthless or the child who is unable to measure up to the parents' expectations may take drastic measures to relieve his or her pain and suffering.

The hope of any society is in its children. If we as a people continue to tolerate the violence, irresponsible drug usage, immorality, and corrupt governmental, religious and business leadership that seed child abuse, the guilt for sowing a damaged population will be ours. We must, as individuals, reorder our personal priorities and influence local, state and federal governments to increase their aid to the cause of children. It is not enough to give lip service, gasp or express horror at the plight of abused and neglected children. Each and every one of us must get involved by assuming a responsible role in our homes, families, neighborhoods and communities to ensure a healthier future generation.

In looking back, I think the tragedy of preventable damages to children came most acutely to my attention while working as a pediatrician at two different state schools for the mentally and physically handicapped. Seeing so many children, year after year, lying totally disabled in near vegetative conditions as a result of brain damage from beatings, near-drowning, maternal German measles, Rh blood incompatibility or preventable genetic diseases has left a lasting impression upon me. What can one do to prevent these conditions in other children? Perhaps, with this book and your support, we can help make the nineties truly the "decade of the child."

CHAPTER 1

FROM TIME IMMEMORIAL

HISTORICAL OVERVIEW OF
CHILD ABUSE AND NEGLECT

Throughout the centuries, children have been willfully killed, maimed, abused and neglected at the hands of rulers, society or parents. Infanticide and abortion have always been a means of population control. Infanticide was prevalent in ancient times and exists today in some primitive and isolated societies. As a baby, Moses was secured in a reed basket and floated down the Nile in old Egypt to escape a mandated death proclaimed by the pharaoh for all male infants. Herod the Great ordered the massacre of children in an attempt to kill the child, Jesus, who threatened his power. Since the fifth century, Christian churches have commemorated this event in one way or another by the Feast of the Holy Innocents—as children slaughtered by Herod were considered the first Christian martyrs. In seventeenth-century England, children were whipped on "Innocents' Day" morning before getting out of bed. (Whether it was to impress the children with reverence for the fatally tragic event or to remind them of how fortunate they were to be alive since Jesus was spared it is difficult to say.) Rome's Christian emperor, Constantine, outlawed infanticide in the fourth century, but the practice continued on into the nineteenth century.

Recently in New York City, a newborn baby boy was found in a plastic trash bag on the street; in a small midwestern town, a college girl attempted to get rid of her unwanted premature baby by flushing him down the dormitory toilet; in Los Angeles, a one-month-old baby was found abandoned in a small, filthy apartment; and in Dallas, still another infant was murdered by drowning in the kitchen sink. And so it goes!

ABORTION

Most religions have rejected induced abortion (the willful termination of pregnancy before the fetus is able to live independently outside the womb), usually with vehemence. They disregard the fact that abortion has been a common method of birth control for unwanted pregnancy throughout history. Men and women, ignorant or irresponsible, ruled by their own passion or pleasure principle, dictated to by the laws of their religion, country or culture, have procreated babies that they would not or could not nurture. Abortion has been intermittently legal or illegal in various nations for almost 200 years. It was not until the nineteenth century that religious leaders began to compel governments to enact criminal penalties against induced abortions. In 1920, the postrevolutionary Soviet Union became the first nation to authorize abortion at the mother's request; sixteen years later, the Soviet Union rescinded the abortion decree; and no less than nineteen years later, abortion became legal again. In the late 1940s, Japan and some Eastern European countries legally sanctioned induced abortion at the pregnant woman's request. By the 1960s and 1970s, Great Britain and some Western European countries (such as Scandinavia and Switzerland) along with certain states in this country broadened their positions on legalizing abortion. Because of the moral issues surrounding abortion and the interpretation of when life begins, much controversy exists today in the United States regarding a woman's right to have an abortion—especially if it is government funded.

INFANTICIDE

Infanticide for unhealthy babies was common practice in ancient Sparta, Greece. Such babies were carried to the top of a mountain and simply thrown off to their certain death. Early Roman custom encouraged abandoning malformed infants in the wilderness to die from exposure, starvation or to be devoured by wild animals. Throughout the ages, all over the world, sickly or deformed babies have been set aside in homes or hospital nurseries to die without benefit of nutrients, proper care, medications or corrective surgery.

GENOCIDE

Whatever happens to the adult population (be it famine, poverty, self-inflicted violence, substance abuse, unemployment or genocide) usually affects the children to an even greater extent. The reverberations are felt for one or more generations, and thus it has been for Jews. Genocide is defined as the systematic, planned annihilation of a racial, religious, political or cultural group. Most vivid in our memory is Adolf Hitler's Holocaust in which the Nazi regime (1933–45) murdered or attempted to exterminate the entire European Jewish population. As a result of this ghastly action, the United Nations in 1946 recognized that "genocide is a crime under international law which the civilized world condemns." Subsequently, the UN Convention on Prevention and Punishment of the Crime of Genocide defined genocide to be any of the following acts perpetrated on a group:

(1) Killing members;

(2) Causing serious bodily or mental harm to members;

(3) Deliberately inflicting on the group conditions of life calculated to bring about its physical destruction in whole or in part;

(4) Imposing measures intended to prevent births within the group; or

(5) Forcibly transferring children of the group to another group.

Unfortunately, like several other issues that the United Nation has addressed, genocide is an international crime by definition only and is not prosecuted. No international court was ever convened.

For my purposes in discussing child abuse and neglect, the preceding definitions of genocide have relevance; each and every one of them is demonstrated in various forms of child abuse and neglect. Although an international criminal court is lacking, the United Nations affirmed by its proclamation that the crime of genocidal acts is an international, not merely a domestic, matter. Doesn't the 1978 mesmerized mass murder-suicide by poisoning of adults and children in Jonestown, Guyana, under the rule of the Reverend Jim Jones qualify as genocide? Doesn't the harsh seduction, control and transport of teenage male and female prostitutes qualify under the acts? Doesn't the "kiddie" pornography industry qualify? Doesn't the white female international sex slavery trade qualify? What about Iraq's President Saddam Hussein's treatment of the Kuwaitis and the Iraqui Kurds?

Famine, imposed or exaggerated by forces other than nature, can be considered a form of genocide perpetrated by "human" rulers. In contrast to nature's potato blight of 1846 in Ireland, causing the starvation and death of one million people (12.5

percent of the eight million population), I cite the early to mid-1900s agricultural collectivization in the Ukraine, enforced by Joseph Stalin's dictum to export grain stocks elsewhere despite the famine. The result was death for 10,000 peasants. What about the current famine in Ethiopia, made worse by the Ethiopian ruling powers that deliberately obstruct distribution of the food and medicine contributed by charitable countries and nonprofit organizations to the victims of the famine? Not only is an entire population starving and suffering, but for younger children who survive, the effect of malnutrition upon their physical and mental development is devastating. (As a pediatrician, I am acutely aware of the deleterious effects of protein deprivation on cerebral development and function.) Since the critical period for brain development is generally considered to be between birth and the age of four years, the irreversible damage done to these malnourished babies is a result of this unconscionable action on the part of Ethiopian leaders. Those children that do survive could scarcely be productive adult members of their society. Is it genocide? Yes. Is it a crime? Yes. Ironically, the fertility rate of starving species increases so that the unhampered birthrate in poor, undeveloped countries (such as India, Africa and much of South America) escalates; babies are born to suffer and die from starvation and disease.

CHILD SACRIFICE

Child sacrifice to the altars of multiple gods pervades world history, sometimes perpetrated for personal salvation or good fortune, other times to bless the crops. It was a tradition in Peru for women to be strangled; in Mayan Mexico, young women were sacrificed by drowning in sacred wells. In fourteenth-century Mexico, Aztec and other Nahuatl infants were sacrificed to the gods when the maize (corn) was planted, and older children were sacrificed when the crops came up. Many cultures (such as Egypt, China, India and Tibet) practiced human sacrifice in different ways until children were replaced by animal, vegetable, or inanimate offerings.

Religious sects practicing cruelty or sacrifice of children have existed throughout the ages. In prehistoric times, river bridge building included the practice of placing humans in the bridge foundations as sacrifices to the river gods. In ancient Vedic, Indian worshipers of the goddess Kali sacrificed a male child once a week on the appointed evening; children were burned in Assyrian and Canaanite rituals and periodically throughout Israelite history. Carthaginians in Phoenicia (now Syria and Lebanon) sacrificed children to the god Baal by burning them, a fact verified by excavators finding burnt bones within buried urns. The practice of child sacrifice persisted in areas of North Africa for many years after Carthage was destroyed by the Romans in 146 B.C. Pre-Columbian Mexican sacramental rituals embodied biannual human sacrifice to the god Huitzilopochtli wherein an image of the god was sculpted with seed, honey and corn, elegantly robed, and transported to the pyramid-temple, where human victims were added to the communion. Replicas of the image were eaten as the flesh and bones of Huitzilopochtli. In the alternate ceremony, the blood of children was added to the replica mixture for consumption. Very similar sacramental rituals were carried out by the Natchez Indians and the Creeks in the southern US regions at corn harvest time. Almost every society has attempted to win favor from a deity by making sacramental offerings—human, animal, vegetable or mineral.

CORPORAL PUNISHMENT

To punish is to inflict pain or any evil upon a wrongdoer. Traditionally, punishment of children has been acceptable if a legitimate relationship exists between the one punishing and the one receiving the punishment. Therefore, for centuries, a parent had not only the right but the obligation to punish his child for whatever he considered a wrongdoing. Different times and cultures have determined which behaviors were acceptable for children and which were punishable. The avoidance of physical punishment as practiced by parents and recommended by child psychologists today would have shocked parents of earlier times. Prior to the 1960s, parental discipline often took the form of physical punishment. When spankings became beatings, physical abuse prevailed. Based upon the head of household and family concept of a parent owning and being responsible for raising his children, surrogate parental roles were placed upon church fathers and school authorities. Consequently, the public acceptance of adults other than a legitimate relative of the child permitted a patriarchal/matriarchal figure to deal out punishment. In Victorian times, children of the upper and middle classes were physically punished for laziness, disobedience, disrespect of elders, any sign of sexual curiosity or self-stimulation, including masturbation and almost anything that offended their parents. Physical abuse of children under the guise of discipline was often considered "preventive medicine" in the United States' colonial history. The Puritans sincerely believed that children, especially boys, needed whippings regularly to "drive out the devil." Corporal punishment for the obstinate or misbehaving child had been widely accepted by parents, schools and church ministers until quite recently. Today nearly all states prohibit physical punishment of public school children.

In my early school years, I distinctly recall several instances of "rowdy" classmates disappearing into the school principal's office to receive their physical punishment. My friend's brother, a fourth grader, stands out in my mind for receiving bloodied knuckles from the principal's ruler. This nine-year-old would then get another beating from his father just "for good measure."

In certain present-day cult communes and Christian private schools, it is standard practice to beat, lock up or deprive children of food for "justifiable" reasons.

MUTILATION

During the 1800s in London, poor parents maimed and crippled their children in order to gain a competitive advantage in sympathy arousal as they turned them out onto the streets to beg. In old China, the custom was to bind the feet of a female child; while the purpose was cosmetic, this practice resulted in deformed feet and painfully difficult walking. Circumcision for hygienic or medical purposes was popular in the United States until about ten years ago; can circumcision be a form of "maiming"?

If one accepts the definition that to maim is to mutilate (injure by removing a bodily part or to disable), there are many examples to be noted throughout history (and even currently): in medieval times, the male foreskin of the penis was fastened and in Rome, the female labia tied together with clasps or stitches, both procedures a form of birth control; removal of the testes was a common form of castration; clitorectomy was practiced in some cultures; disfigurement of heads, nose, ears and lips have been recorded in parts of Africa, Australia and the South Pacific Islands.

SLAVERY AND THE SELLING OF CHILDREN

Both slavery and the selling of children for various purposes have permeated the history of man. Records indicate that children of Babylonia and Egypt in the second century B.C. were sold into slavery by their debtor parents. In ancient Greece, abandoned children of poor parents taken in by others to feed and raise were considered their slaves. Constantine the Great sanctioned the sale of newborns. In A.D. 1212, a valiant movement by thousands of Christian European children, who were determined to take back the Holy Land from the Muslims nonviolently, ended in tragic failure. An estimated forty to fifty thousand children were captured and sold by avaricious adults into slavery. The failed movement, originating in France and Germany and at one time led by a ten-year-old boy, is known as "the Children's Crusade." Some historians think it was the motivator for the Fifth Crusade of 1217. From the eighteenth through the nineteenth centuries, the selling of children was not uncommon in those families with too many mouths to feed. "Farming out" of boys and girls alike was frequently accompanied by their exploitation.

Thousands of children, disabled or of minority extraction, abused or abandoned, live in institutions, community group residences or one foster home after another until they are of majority age (or forever)—never knowing an exclusive parent-child relationship.

CHILD LABOR

The Industrial Revolution in this country and abroad generated child labor sweatshops. Deprived of education or just having the time to be kids, children were expected to contribute to the family's support. Again, the children of the poor were the victims of abuse and slave labor. During the Great Depression, poor children working in factories and mills were joined by their many middle-class peers whenever menial work was available. Labor rights legislation was slow in coming to the United States, and child protection laws were not enacted until the Fair Labor Standards Act was passed in 1938.

Nor have child labor abuses disappeared today. In a short, intensive nationwide search with approximately 3,400 investigations, the US Department of Labor found 7,000 cases of child labor law violations (Mashek et al. 1990).

MODERN TIMES

Added to the historical forms of child abuse are the current ones: prenatal abuses, drug-addicted parents and pornographic exploitation. The increased frequency of teenage motherhood (children raising children), divorced parents, spouse-child kidnapping and single mothers living in isolation from family support lay the groundwork and increase the risk for child abuse and neglect.

The escalation of overt violence in our homes, on our streets and in school playing fields is out of control. Average people have come to tolerate violence in their daily lives. Why else would we accept the media moguls making millions of dollars by television and movie depictions of violence that we so avidly watch and fund? Even some Saturday morning cartoons, watched by children as young as two years old, demonstrate brutal acts as entertainment. An impressionable young mind cannot distinguish between fiction and reality. The child becomes confused, has nightmares or mimics an injurious assault while innocently failing to comprehend the consequences.

Child rights advocates in government, law, sociology, education and medicine have made great strides over the past twenty years. In particular, the Child Abuse Prevention and Treatment Act of 1974 was major legislation toward the protection of children against abuse and neglect. However, the proliferation of wrongs against the helpless in the very late twentieth century is proof that we are not doing enough! Will we come full circle and repeat past history in the treatment of our children?

The 1990s may not be devoid of the "sale of children." Lest we think that the selling of children was relegated to the past, modern-day incidents are emerging. Infertile childless couples, frustrated by the scarcity of so-called "desirable" healthy Caucasian infants and by the endless waiting period for approved adoption agencies, turn to other means of acquiring a child. They pay dearly for surrogate mothers, privately negotiated adoptions or for children from overseas. It is paradoxical that while so many unwanted, needy children live dismal lives in the United States, these waifs are not among those considered "adoptable."

CHAPTER 2

PLIGHT OF THE INNOCENT

SEXUAL ABUSE

All but the most severe forms of sexual abuse tend to go unidentified, and yet the experts estimate that one out of every three or four girls and one out of every seven to ten boys below the age of eighteen are violated. The US Department of Health and Human Services (US DHHS) describes three categorical forms of sexual abuse (US DHHS 1988, 4–5):

INTRUSION: evidence of actual penile penetration—whether oral, anal, or genital, homosexual or heterosexual;

MOLESTATION WITH GENITAL CONTACT: acts where some form of actual genital contact had occurred, but where there was no specific indication of intrusion;

OTHER OR UNKNOWN SEXUAL ABUSE: unspecified acts not known to have involved actual genital contact (e.g. fondling of breasts or buttocks, exposure) and for allegations concerning inadequate or inappropriate supervision of a child's voluntary sexual activities.

The national incidence of reported sexual abuse tripled from 1980 to 1986. According to the statisticians, it was largely attributable to better reporting, but who knows? The very nature of the subject is so repulsive to most of us that open discussion is generally muffled. The victims are too ashamed to speak out. Reportedly, child sexual abuse ranks third in the prevalence of all abuses after physical and emotional abuse. Whatever service professionals, researchers or bureaucratic agencies label as a particular form of child abuse or neglect is arbitrary. Maltreatment is abuse, be it physical or sexual. The everlasting effect is psychological.

Pedophilia (from the Greek, meaning love of children) commonly refers to the practice of deriving sexual gratification from prepubertal children. Most often the act is fondling, inducing the youngster to handle the pedophile's genitals; less frequently, the act is sadistic, involving sodomy or rape. No matter what the form, pedophilia is a heinous crime. It is a violation of a child's body by a predator who bribes, intimidates and coerces the helpless, unsophisticated child for his own purpose. Veiled in secrecy, the pedophile, nearly always male, may be a judge, teacher, doctor, religious leader, athletic coach or police officer; even a father, stepfather, brother, uncle or grandfather. Who is going to suspect such a person? And yet, right under our noses, the pedophile plots his scheme of entrustment by the child. When accomplished, he seizes the opportunity to pounce. So much for the commonly held myth that a mentally retarded male or a "dirty old man" is the most likely to harm a child—it does happen, but rarely.

OUT OF SILENCE

As the whole subject of pedophilia and incest emerges from a century of black holes, persons in their thirties, forties, and beyond are speaking out. These women and men reveal in psychotherapy or in self-help groups such as Alcoholics Anonymous (AA) the damage that occurred years before by an incident (or several episodes) of sexual abuse. Blocked from their memories are whole periods of their childhood. They have unexplainable feelings of guilt or shame, disdain for their bodies, and feelings of inadequacy in sexual relationships. Some adults come to counseling with histories of repetitive depression; food, drug, gambling or alcohol addictions; and other self-destructive behavior. Phobias, anxiety reactions or hypochondria are frequent. Common to nearly all is a sense of low self-value.

BARBARA————————————————————————

Barbara was an attractive woman of twenty-nine who had repressed her childhood sexual abuse for years. She had thrown herself into postgraduate academic pursuits after acquiring a bachelor's degree, two master's degrees and finally a doctorate in microbiology—to the exclusion of all but platonic relationships. It wasn't until a prolonged hospital stay for severe postpartum depression that her story unfolded. Having reached twenty-eight, feeling lonely and desperate but at the same time abhorring the idea of a marital commitment, she decided that she wanted to have a baby. Her solution was to have intercourse with her brightest and most handsome undergraduate student. It wasn't all that difficult for Barbara to seduce this macho kid who was flattered that someone of her stature would be interested. The hot and furious affair lasted until her pregnancy test was positive, at which point she dropped him. Being a pregnant single woman in a large university presented no problem among her peers, but she, herself, became progressively more anxious and ambivalent about having the child.

After her baby girl was born, Barbara dropped into a deep depression requiring intensive psychiatric help. During the course of her therapy, she talked about dreaming of a small girl being sexually molested; she thought that the girl was herself or maybe it was her daughter and that maybe her baby girl would be better off dead. Family history indicated that her biological father was killed in an auto accident before Barbara was born. Her stepfather, a college professor, had been an integral part of her rearing. Because of his teaching schedule, he was at home alone with her more often than her nine-to-five working mother. Was this merely circumstantial evidence as to the identity of her abuser? Barbara was never able to confront or openly accuse him; her stepfather had died years ago of a heart attack and her mother of cancer. Continual therapy was effective in psychologically enabling her to raise her baby and resume her career, but a sustained, intimate heterosexual relationship was not to be within her capability.

FETISHISM AND SADISM

Adult sexual deviations, including sadism, masochism, rape, exhibitionism, voyeurism, pedophilia and fetishism, appear to be the result of sexual maldevelopment during the early formative years. The impact is for life. Sadism exists as a basic motivator of wife, girlfriend and child beaters. Who could be more innocent or vulnerable to sexual molestation than an infant with Down's syndrome? This is the story of Terry, whom I had seen in the Child Development Clinic in Boston.

TERRY————————————————————————

Terry was brought in by his parents, Terrence and Mary Flanagan, and their priest. They were referred for confirmation of his Down's syndrome diagnosis and counseling. Down's syndrome is a relatively common genetic disorder caused by having an extra chromosome and resulting in mental retardation and physical anomalies. Unless children with this condition have a serious heart or bowel defect, they do quite well and are characteristically affable, happy persons.

As the five of us sat in my examining room, I could see how emotionally devastated this couple was by Terry's condition. Mary Flanagan was on the brink of tears as she held her baby rather stiffly away from her body, indicating to me the sorrow and lack of acceptance she felt for her three-month-old. Mr. Flanagan gazed off in the distance without making eye contact with anybody. The priest merely listened as a supportive silent observer.

Terry was the firstborn of this attractive couple in their mid-twenties. He had all the classic features of Down's: Mongoloid face with slanted eyes, short nose and small, low-set ears. I could hear no heart murmur, which presumably meant that he did not have a heart defect. In general, he appeared to be quite healthy. Chromosome analysis had revealed that he did have the extra chromosome (Number 21), indicating Down's syndrome.

On the first visit, it was my primary job to confirm and explain the diagnosis relative to its significance in Terry's future. While he would always have developmental delays, a lag in walking and speech would be the most obvious symptoms in early childhood. The Child Development Center (CDC) could offer an intervention program for him as soon as he became one year old or so. The child development therapist and the pediatric physical therapist would instruct the mother on stimulation techniques at each stage of his development.

Although Mr. and Mrs. Flanagan seemed encouraged by our informational session, I sensed that they would need a lot of ongoing support until such time that they could accept Terry's condition and cope with it. Two months later, I saw Terry accompanied by Mary and her mother, Mrs. Leary. Terry was fine but his parents' marriage was not. His father had moved out. Mary, not being able to manage alone with her small baby, had moved in with her mother. Mr. Flanagan had become very depressed by the mere sight of his retarded son for whom he had held so many aspirations. Mrs. Leary offered her overwrought, insecure daughter experienced parenting and companionship.

Subsequently, Mrs. Leary called to tell me that Mary had been committed to a mental health hospital after a suicide attempt: her husband had filed for divorce.

It was not until Terry was a year old that Mrs. Leary returned with him to the CDC. He had grown nicely and was making the expected developmental progress. Her main concern was his patchy loss of scalp hair and swollen red penis. He had become very irritable and a poor sleeper. She told me that the bald spots had increased during the past month and his swollen red penis was noticed off and on during the same period. After ruling out organic disease causes for his problems, I questioned her at length about the sequence of events in Terry's life. It seems that following Mary's return home from the mental health hospital, she had started to date a single, middle-aged dentist. She and Terry had been spending weekends at his luxurious home for the past month. Since Mary had been taking more care of her baby recently, Mrs. Leary had not especially noticed the correlation between the baby's hair and penile conditions and the weekend visits. As soon as I suspected a possible connection, I asked our social worker to join us in order to gain Mrs. Leary's confidence. A home visit was arranged with Mary to gather more firsthand information.

Our horrid suspicions were confirmed by Mary. The boyfriend, during those Saturdays and Sundays while Terry was sleeping at his home, would masturbate Terry's penis and simultaneously pull out tiny pinches of his hair. Apparently, Mary just stood by, sacrificing her son for her sick lover's pleasure.

The social worker took action and contacted Mary's mental health professionals and the child protective agencies. (By law, social workers and physicians, among others, must report knowledge of child abuse. Basically, it was not our intention to punish these two abusers through the courts but to prevent any further abuse.) Mary's second suicide attempt within a year necessitated an indefinite institutional stay. With the threat of a potential scandal and legal action, the dentist suddenly closed his office and departed the state for extended foreign travel.

Like a "good Gramma," Mrs. Leary assumed full care of her grandson. Terry's hair grew in and his penis returned to normal; he became the happy, nonirritable, well-sleeping child that he was supposed to be. Gramma and he attended the CDC regularly. We observed him to be making excellent developmental progress.

For us, the main thing left to do was to ensure Terry a loving and nonabusive upbringing in which he could thrive. The social worker, Mrs. Graves, and I met with the local and state child protective representatives and mental health agents in order to discuss the best possible home situation for Terry. Everyone's personal and professional repugnance of his past abusive experiences had to be put aside. (What benefit would it have been to Terry for us to pursue public exposure, legal charges and punishment of the deviant dentist? He was gone from the community and Terry's mentally ill mother was receiving therapy in her confinement. Under the circumstances, the district attorney would not elect to accept this case.) All agreed that Mrs. Leary would be her grandson's best caretaker. No one could dispute her track record for sustained interest in Terry, despite her daughter's problems. Our recommendations were implemented when she accepted guardianship and subsequently was permitted to adopt Terry.

Psychiatric speculation might interpret the dentist abuser as using Terry as a fetish, an inanimate object from which he derived sexual excitement. Perhaps he was a sadist. Whether practicing fetishism or sadism, the activity represented sexual deviation thought to be deeply seated in his childhood maldevelopment. Theories regarding the causative factors in fetishism range from the psychoanalytic focus on the Oedipus complex and fears of penile castration to conditioning or imprinting sexual arousal to an inanimate neutral object very early in life. A sadist is one who derives sexual excitement through inflicting physical pain on a human or animal. The dentist's actions were quite possibly a combination of both fetishism and sadism. Sexual deviations (such as pedophilia, sadism or fetishism) like other forms of abuse traverse intellectual, socioeconomic, racial and age boundaries.

DAY-CARE CENTERS

Infamous cases of sexual molestation in day-care centers as broadcast by the media have made parents frantic over what types of persons and facilities they should entrust with their child's well-being. Most parents these days need a two-spouse income and, if not, many women choose to pursue their professional careers or outside-of-the-home jobs because they feel more fulfilled. More often than not, these women are convinced that they are better quality-time mothers as a result. There are no guarantees on the safety and enrichment of one's child. Each parent must decide, according to his or her will, conscience and circumstances, how and who will care for the child. For the all-too-frequent single parent who has to work, day-care is not optional. (With minimal reservation, I think that the opportunity for a preschooler, ages two to five, to interrelate with other children in a group setting is a vital experience in psychosocial development. Mothers and fathers, get off your guilt trip!) Day-care is the normal thing for this generation of children. It's here to stay.

This is not to say that parents should be unconcerned about their child being exposed to persons that might sexually molest them. Eighty-five percent of reported cases occur with a male perpetrator familiar to the child; more than half of these are family members, not strangers. Most incidents are known to take place insidiously in a homey private setting. Parents of day-care children should remember an old adage, "There is safety in numbers." In fact, day-care centers may be a safer place than your home in avoiding child injuries. A recent study indicated that injuries (minor and major) requiring medical attention were twice as frequent in the home versus the day-care center (Rivara et al. 1989, 1011–1016). The significance of this medical report tends to justify local and state governmental regulations licensing day-care facilities, despite the resultant extra costs for child care. (As a pediatrician, mother and grandmother, I would like to see greater attention paid to the qualifications for direct child care personnel. Undoubtedly, it would mean higher wages, but it should result in greater quality of care and stability of staff.)

HARRIET

Harriet was a two-year-old whose working parents had enrolled her in a well-recommended and licensed day-care center after a careful screening of the staff. After her initial day or two of demonstrating separation anxiety from her parents, she was reported by the staff to have made a good adjustment. Like many female two-year-olds, she was completely toilet trained but required assistance wiping her bottom.

Three months down the road from Harriet's entrance into the day-care program, she started to resist her father's assistance at home with her toilet activities, especially the wiping part. At day-care, she intermittently wet or soiled her panties. Parents and day-care staff conferred to search out a cause for Harriet's relapse in toilet training and resistance to her father's assistance. Several days' careful observation of her behavior at day-care ensued. An astute observer found a hint as to the cause of the problem: a new male staff member would jump to assist with Harriet's toileting whenever the female staff were busy. Although unprovable, the assumption was that he was massaging her genitoanal area during the wiping process after urination and defecation. Despite the fellow's good credentials and work performance, he was suspected of pedophilia and promptly fired. Harriet gradually reassumed her complete toilet training record and for a while her father backed off at home from assisting her.

THE MENTALLY ILL OR RETARDED CHILD

Numerous cases of sexual molestation on female residents of institutions for the mentally ill or retarded have been reported in-house. The victims have usually been abused by male residents or staff. Not infrequently, the sexually molested have become pregnant. In the case that follows, the sexual assault occurred in a community placement foster home.

Joan had been caught up in the court mandates to empty the institutions at all costs. The philosophical idea behind providing more normalized living environments for the disabled was sound. Unfortunately, many of the placements met only the minimal bureaucratic standards for health and safety and did not provide the emotional support that was needed to enhance the lives of the disabled.

JOAN———————————————————————————

Joan was a tall, full-figured, barely verbal fifteen-year-old with a mental age of six. She had been at a state school (where I was on the staff) since her mother died and her father remarried. Joan attended a special education program at a large high school some twenty-five miles away, meaning that she was only on the state school campus nights, holidays and weekends. The significance to our story was that our multidisciplinary daytime staff rarely saw Joan. In fact, I only saw her for her annual physical exam. All systems, including her guardian's consent for foster home placement and discharge from the school, were ready. She was to live with a couple named Smythe who had two children of their own and lived in a tidy house in the country. Her schooling was to continue as before. The staff was very much in favor of her moving to a family setting.

It was Easter Sunday morning, some three months after her departure, when she was abruptly returned to us. Joan looked physically fine, not confused or agitated. So, why was she sent back?

Subsequently, we learned that while sitting at breakfast with her new family, Joan suddenly lunged across the table at Mr. Smythe and tried to gouge his eyes. He sought emergency room treatment for minimal trauma and notified the authorities of the incident. He demanded that they remove Joan from his house immediately. Since she was nonverbal, nobody ever heard her side of the story.

Speculation abounded about what had provoked this mild, almost placid girl to attack Mr. Smythe. She had never exhibited violent behavior before. A readmission physical exam had been perfectly normal, giving me no clue as to what might have taken place during her absence from us. Following a week's observation in our infirmary, Joan returned to her previous dorm living quarters. She resumed her public schooling.

Several weeks later I received a call from the nursing staff who questioned why she was gaining weight despite her caloric reduction diet. They had searched for the most likely cause: cheating with high-caloric junk food obtained off-campus. Without an organic disease reason for her weight gain, I recommended continuation of her diet and more physical activity. Any exercise was an improvement over her usual sedentary habit. Time passed but only further weight gain occurred. (My prescription was not working and I was soon to discover why.) Daytime, evening and night nurses compiled their data, which indicated no record of Joan having had a menstrual period since her return to us three months previously. What had I missed? How obvious it would have been to suspect anyone but Joan.

Her pregnancy test was positive. Had she shown even the slightest interest in sexual activity, we would not have been so surprised. An obstetrician reaffirmed her pregnancy, judging it to be about eighteen weeks. Another week went by before I could reach her vacationing public guardian, Ms. Chatt. It would be the guardian's decision as to whether or not Joan would carry her pregnancy to term. Ms. Chatt, the state school administrator, the obstetrician and I met to discuss Joan's situation: her maternal risks for complications and the risks to the fetus for mental retardation or birth defects. Although Joan was healthy, she had a convulsive disorder that required Tegretol for seizure control. Tegretol worked very well for Joan, but like most anticonvulsant drugs, it had been implicated in birth defect causality. The other risk to the fetus was a genetic condition, inherent in the suspected father. Mr. Smythe was an achondroplastic dwarf, the most commonly occurring type of dwarfism. This condition carries a risk of 50 percent to any offspring conceived by a dwarf of being a dwarf. Joan's mental retardation per se, without a known genetic cause, could not be considered a predictable risk for the fetus. Her mental incompetence and life long dependency upon a caretaker herself would hamper her from rearing a child independently. All of these factors were discussed over and over with Ms. Chatt. She continued to procrastinate. (Joan's old records had shown that this same guardian had procrastinated before about giving Joan birth control pills prior to her going off-campus to high school and later to community placement.) Meanwhile, it was difficult to watch Joan's physical metamorphosis and discomfort, for which she had no understanding.

Finally, after several phone calls to Ms. Chatt, who still could not come to a decision as to what to do with her client, the school administrator and I "threatened" her with a legal and administrative bypass. The guardian opted for the termination of Joan's pregnancy. By that time the pregnancy was twenty weeks, too late for our state to legally allow an abortion.

This indecisive, questionably competent guardian "forced" Joan (with a nurse chaperon) to travel out of state to a university hospital to have the termination. During the forty-eight-hour procedure, the nurse and Joan stayed in a hotel adjacent to the hospital. That night Joan had a rare seizure recurrence. Ultimately, she expelled the uterine contents without complications. Upon her return to our facility, she showed no signs of postpartum depression. Apparently, the abrupt hormonal change had not affected her.

That crisis resolved, the remaining issue for Joan's future protection against unwanted pregnancy would be a decision about some form of birth control. With her return to high school and future community placement, Joan would continue to be vulnerable to sexual assaults that she couldn't report. Knowing Ms. Chatt's track record for "timely" decisions, I again approached her on the subject. I could scarcely believe her lack of response. We all, especially Joan, had been through a terrible ordeal that could be repeated. Nothing about Joan was going to change except the genetic potential of the father of her next pregnancy. Incomprehensible to me was that Ms. Chatt failed to recognize this.

The decision regarding birth control had not been made within the ten months that I remained as Joan's physician before leaving for another job, nor had Ms. Chatt or the authorities prosecuted or even investigated the suspected father and rapist. Let's hope that at least he has been taken off the eligibility list for foster parenting. The bureaucratic gaps and lacks of communication between agencies is so frequent: the system is so complex that all too often child abuse and neglect go along without effective curtailment in spite of our best efforts.

FALSE ACCUSATIONS

The "plight of the innocent" cannot exclusively be confined to the children that have been or will be abused. It also applies to the parent or male caretaker who is falsely accused. Innocent fathers have become suspect because child protectors, well-meaning professionals and legal advocates possess a heightened awareness of sexual molestation. The usual accusers are vindictive, separated or divorced mothers who object to a father's visitation rights or joint child custody. The imaginative, hurt and confused child caught in the middle of the parental break up may be influenced to fabricate stories of sexual molestation. With the escalation of the divorce rate during the 1970s and 1980s, more children and parents encounter acrimonious dissolution of their families. More women who have lost the financial and emotional security of marriage and child rearing have lashed out against the father of their child using any available ammunition. Their intent is to degrade and discredit just as they have been demeaned.

Other than threatened and threatening mothers playing games, some young children, influenced by adult sexual exhibitions on cable television or pornographic tapes, fallaciously report their fathers or male caretakers as performing such acts on them. Although they can scarcely understand the serious repercussions of their references, they receive the gratification of extraordinary attention. Mothers, gullible adults and professionals often use the child's fantasy for their own purposes. Not unique is the preadolescent girl, naively mimicking a female adult role model, which can be interpreted as seductive behavior toward any familiar male (such as father, uncle or grandfather). The harm to the innocent adult male is done as soon as a suspicion is cast.

TANYA

Tanya's father was caught up in a bitter divorce and custody suit when her mother, Lori, accused him of child sexual molestation. Her parents had been married for ten years. Tanya was five years old when the marital and custody crisis surfaced. For sometime before her father had moved out, she had sensed her parents' quiet interpersonal hostility. She missed her daddy's being home to help her in the bathtub, share supper and tuck her into bed. For as long as she could remember, he had always been there for her in the evening. It had become a very special social time for them both. Lori excused his absence by saying that he was working late. In reality, this might have been true. As a busy physician, he could have been tending to patients except for the fact that his employment contract in a medical group required only 8:00 A.M. to 5:00 P.M. hours and no night coverage. More than once, Tanya was awakened late at night by her parents' loud arguments. During the day, she would find her mommy crying. She was frightened by this whole change in her previously happy home; Mommy had no time for her and Daddy was seldom home.

Her parents' divorce agreement called for Tanya to spend stay-over weekends at her father's condominium. For several weeks this arrangement worked well, with Tanya living at home with her mother weekdays and visiting her father on Saturdays and Sundays. It came to an end when Tanya's mother learned that a pretty young lady was living in "Daddy's" condo. That did it! Lori's jealously overwhelmed her. She ranted and raved to her lawyer who advised her that because the divorce was final, her ex-husband had every right to have a live-in girlfriend. In order to withdraw Tanya's visitations with her father, there would have to be a more substantive reason. It was at that point that Lori became alerted to a child molestation case in the newspaper. This charge might provide the grounds she needed to get back at her ex-husband. She cleverly plotted her scheme of revenge. After doing her resource work at the library, she laid the foundation by telling friends and family that Tanya was being sexually molested by her father. By fabricating potentially incriminating statements that Tanya had innocently made, she distorted a previously benign habit of his bathtub supervision and bedtime tucking-in as suggestive of a long-term father-daughter intimacy.

When her new accusations failed to convince her lawyer to petition the court for withdrawal of joint custody and visitations, she found another lawyer who complied with her wishes. The gossip chain kicked-in with other physicians' wives and soon spread to his medical group and the hospital staff. People may excuse adultery and accept divorce but will treat rumors of child sexual molestation very harshly. Ultimately, Lori's charges were denied by the court for insufficient evidence. The pathetic result of her irrational and vindictive plot was that everyone was harmed. Lori lost credibility, friends and lots of money through legal fees; Tanya was subjected to a form of psychological abuse; and her daddy lost his professional reputation, friends, family and his daughter's unrestricted love and trust.

JAKINA

Another instance of false accusation toward an innocent father figure was revealed in Jakina's case. Nine-year-old Jakina's biological father was a truck driver killed in a road accident before she was two. Her mother had a rough time supporting and caring for Jakina and her baby brother. She literally worked all the time—days as a waitress and nights as a cocktail hostess. Jakina's first stepfather, a commercial fisherman, entered her life when she was three years old. She took to him immediately and he treated her like a fairy princess. Although his work required long absences away from home, she loved him dearly as the only father she had ever known. About two years later, she, her brother and her mother were anxiously awaiting his overdue return when his ship arrived without him. He had been washed overboard during a bad storm at sea and was never found. Jakina's mother was emotionally devastated by the death of a second husband. Within a few months, she remarried; this time it was an older man who could provide her and the children with the security of a safe occupation. He was a real estate broker whom her mother had met at her lounge job. Divorced with grown children, the hope was that he would provide the long-term stability that she and the children needed.

In the beginning, Jakina was very slow to accept him, but then she became overly affectionate and quite flirtatious for a six-year-old. She copied her mother's role model with a seductive approach to her new father: sitting on his lap, kissing him on the lips, rumpling his hair and nuzzling his ears and neck. When her mom was out, she tried on her makeup, clothes and stuffed her bras. Jakina was constantly snuggled between her parents on the living room couch, in front of the evening TV and in their bed first thing in the morning. Her behavior did not go unnoticed, just misinterpreted. Because of Jakina's initial reluctance to accept her new stepfather, both parents were delighted to see the change. As the months went by, her mom thought that she was just trying to solidify his love and to ensure that he didn't leave her like the others. Her husband, never having a daughter, thought this was the way all little girls treated their father. Beyond that, he was outright flattered and pleased by her.

When Jakina turned eight and her physical behavior persisted, Mom wondered why she had not outgrown it. She would be the first to admit to her emerging jealousy and resentment toward her daughter, who never seemed to leave her husband alone. The marriage was slipping downhill. In addition to financial troubles, her husband had lost interest in maintaining their sexual relationship. That made her irritable. Her tensions and frustrations erupted: she accused him of sexually molesting her daughter. He of course denied it and insisted that Jakina be psychologically examined. Fortunately, they happened onto a child psychologist experienced in such matters, since many are not and might support the child's fantasies and the mother's paranoid suspicions. Before more harm was done to the husband-wife relationship and the stepfather's reputation, the matter was resolved by the psychologist's negative report. The truth of the matter was that his sexual disinterest was due to his high blood pressure medication, which had caused impotence, a condition he tried to hide from his younger wife. Once the medication was changed, he was able to satisfy them both. With firm notice to Jakina about her behavior being unacceptable, she too overcame what could have been a counterproductive course.

INCEST

For an untold number of women, the effects of incestuous sexual abuse lasts a lifetime. Mrs. Gail Schumaker is such a person. Now about thirty-seven years old, happily married, but regrettably childless, her problem started in childhood.

GAIL————————————————————

Born and reared in an affluent family, she was the oldest of three girls. Her parents, Mr. and Mrs. Trott, were prominent members of the community and well-liked. He was a very successful corporate lawyer; she a talented artist. Despite their many social commitments, they always found time for their children. Weekends and vacations were spent at the shore or the mountains doing things together as a family. Gail was a happy, well-adjusted girl until the age of eleven, when her dad initiated a change in their father-daughter relationship.

His previous affectionate, playful ways became much more intimate. Gradually, his hugs extended to hand-feeling maneuvers of her breasts, bottom and pubic area; his cheek kisses became lip-tongue kisses. His approach was so subtle that Gail never questioned its significance. After all, ever since she could remember, he was the loving and trusted father who had been there to comfort her hurts, have fun with, and provide guidance. His appreciation of her pubertal blossoming was not unpleasant to her. In fact, it was downright flattering and flirtatious. (Gail and her mother had never been close and less so lately. Although Mom provided her with new bras and menstrual tampons, she did not talk about the changes Gail's body was undergoing or the hazards of womanhood.) It was not long before—in Mom's absence, of course—his caresses became more purposeful, simulating foreplay.

Gail recalls that she liked her father's exclusive attention and remarks about how beautiful she was as he gently slipped off her clothes. She was almost twelve before he exposed himself to her. Because she had grown up with sisters only, she had never seen male genitalia in the flesh. Her natural curiosity was shockingly satisfied. Even when sexual intercourse was initiated, he was very gentle. Dad made it clear that their "beautiful" episodes should be kept private—in other words, don't tell anybody, especially your mother. Gail, like the obedient daughter she was, kept their secret for a year.

As his sexual demands increased and he ceased to be gentle, Gail dreaded their encounters. With the newfound social awareness of a thirteen-year-old, she knew his behavior was wrong. She told her mother. Mom did not or chose not to believe her. Why should she? Mrs. Trott had a fine marriage with mutually satisfying sex that hadn't wavered in thirty-six years. This teenage daughter must be fantasizing about her dad. Obviously, she had been contaminated by sexy movies, dirty books or "bad" friends. Gail's emotional swings—screeching in anger, sassing, crying, laughing or stubborn silence—was the kind of behavior any other mother of a teenage daughter might experience.

Gail was devastated by her mother's failure to believe her. Her dad took even greater advantage: she grudgingly submitted to his rapes. Eventually, she lashed out in a most self-destructive manner. She became promiscuous with her male peers at school and other boys around town. Her attitude was, Why not do it with someone of my own choosing? Maybe it would be fun! I'm not a virgin anyway, thanks to my own father, so what more do I have to lose?

As a bright student from a middle- to upper-class family, she was easily accepted at a prestigious college. The fact that it was 3,000 miles away gave her a real out from the attentions of her father and the local boys. College provided her with a whole new life. She enjoyed her courses, female dorm friends and independence. Her sexual activity became very discreet.

However, she was still plagued by a vaginal discharge that she had had since high school. Intermittent treatment had not cured her. One day she became acutely ill with unrelenting abdominal pain. The emergency room physician diagnosed pelvic inflammatory disease (PID). PID is usually caused by gonorrhea, which can spread from vagina to uterus to fallopian tubes (the connectors to the ovaries). Intensive treatment with antibiotics cured her, but the physicians failed to impress upon her that the infection could have scarred her tubes, leaving her infertile. (Gonorrhea, one of the common venereal diseases, used to be treated easily by penicillin before a resistant strain of bacteria emerged. Left inadequately treated, gonorrhea infects and scars female tubes and leads to blockage, thus preventing fertilization of the egg.)

Gail graduated with honors in economics and found a top job on Wall Street. It was there that she met her future husband, Larry. A twelve month courtship ensued without premarital sex. She had found a man who could share her every interest and love without physical demands. Even at her wedding, her dad's gaze was lustful. She wondered if her younger sisters had been his victims since her departure from home. There was never an opportunity to ask them. Her experience was too painful to relate, even to her husband. Her mom continued to be blissfully ignorant in denying her accusations.

For years, Gail and her husband tried to conceive a child. During the course of her fertility studies, when I first met her, the diagnosis was confirmed that her tubes were badly scarred. There was no way that her husband's sperm could reach her egg for fertilization. Pregnancy would be impossible without gynecological manipulations. Gail and Larry were willing to try anything to have a child of their own. Over a period of sixty months, Gail endured one surgical procedure after another to repair her tubes, to artificially fertilize her eggs with Larry's sperm, and to implant the same into her uterus. All medical attempts were unsuccessful in creating a viable pregnancy. Emotionally and financially depleted, they gave up as Gail's biological clock ran out. The earlier years of incestuous sexual abuse and promiscuity had deprived her of natural motherhood.

DETECTING THE SIGNS

In order to detect the possible signs of child sexual abuse or molestation, parents, caretakers and teachers must *listen* to the child and *note changes* in his or her behavior. When a child suddenly voices an aversion toward someone or some place, including a separated parent or their home, the charge warrants investigating. The subtle signs for the young child may be: inappropriately seductive behavior; nightmares; bed-wetting; trouble falling asleep without the new requirement of a night-light or extra comforting; or abrupt fear of being alone or separating from the parent. The blatant signs are: prepubertal blood staining of underpants; fecal soiling or resistance toward having a bowel movement; vaginal discharge that tests positive for a sexually transmitted disease and unexplained scratching of the genital area. A good thing for the parent or caretaker to do is take the child for a thorough examination of his or her genital area, being careful to choose a gentle and tactful physician who will not further frighten the youngster.

CHARLIE————————————————————————

A second-grade teacher noticed that Charlie came into her classroom quietly with a straddling gait, quite different from his usual robust, noisy entry with strutting gait. Throughout the morning Charlie squirmed in his seat, rejected her verbal requests to participate in classroom activities, and finally ran out to the hall. The school principal found him hiding in the boy's toilet.

The male principal literally dragged the child, kicking and yelling profanities, to the health office. Charlie was "frightened to death." The school nurse was just about to leave for her next school assignment when the child ran to her, embraced her with tight hugs, and broke down completely with incessant weeping. She was able to discover what was hurting him, at least physically: Charlie was bleeding from his anus and his entire penis and scrotum were red and raw. Like most little kids, he was not going to tell her, or even his mother, who had done it to him. Upon learning of his condition, his mother suspected her live-in boyfriend. He had arrived home late the night before so drunk and enraged about losing his job that she left the apartment rather than take the abuse. Her son took it for her—brutally.

It didn't have to be a boyfriend who abused Charlie, it could have been an out-of-control husband, ex-spouse or any male who was himself hurting and "disturbed."

MARIA

When three-year-old Maria came bursting through the ajar bathroom door one Sunday morning, catching her daddy standing naked outside the shower stall, he was somewhat embarrassed. She stared briefly at his genitals. When she suddenly lurched forward, grabbing his penis, he was more than a little shocked. As he released her grasp, he yelled, "What the hell are you doing?" Maria began to sob and cried out, "Daddy, I love you! I love you!" Mom ran up from the kitchen where she had been making blueberry pancakes for their special Sunday breakfast. The rest of the day was consumed by trying to figure out why Maria had done such a thing. The only clue derived was from Maria sobbing repeatedly, "Love Mommy, love Daddy, love Uncle Tony." Indeed, Uncle Tony (her father's brother, divorced and living alone, who was always available to baby-sit Maria when they couldn't find a local teenage girl) became their prime suspect as a pedophile. After some pretty heavy strong-arm tactics by his brother, Tony confessed to fondling Maria and having her stroke his penis. He denied any oral, anal or vaginal invasions. Unbeknownst to Maria's parents, such activities were the reasons why he did not get the custody of his own children after his divorce. The pediatrician confirmed a lack of evidence of vaginal or anal trauma in Maria; a child psychologist could find no immediately detectable trauma. She advised the parents to watch and wait for signs of psychological damage rather than to project their adult interpretation of the little girl's experiences. (A three-year-old child who is caressed and caresses someone they love does not recognize such behavior as sexual molestation; that connotation is given by anxious parents and adults, professionals included, and, in fact, creates moralistic emotional trauma in the child.) Despite the psychologist's advice, Maria's parents became so sensitized to the potential of their daughter being sexually molested again that they found it extremely difficult to entrust her to anyone's care. The issue made for a very abnormal condition, affecting both parents and child and nearly wrecking their marriage.

CAUSATION AND PREVENTION

The incidence of sexual abuse and molestation among American children and youth is outrageous. Educated "guess-timates" indicate that one out of every three or four girls and one out of every seven to ten boys under age eighteen are sexually molested. These figures may be conservative. The onset can occur in infancy, as in the case of Terry, or at anytime throughout childhood and adolescence. Sexual abuse/molestation is often difficult to detect. Even when suspected, this form of child abuse is frequently covered up or denied entirely by the family of the victim. The older child who is able to recognize the wrongfulness of such acts may be unwilling to communicate his or her abuses to family or outside sources for potential help. The reasons are complex, both real and psychological: fear of retribution via increased intimidation from the abuser; fear of loss of affection and financial support from a father or stepfather; fear of rejection by mother for accusations against her husband, boyfriend or brother; and, finally, the terrible internal shame and guilt about the whole situation in which one was a participant. The mentally retarded child like Joan, the emotionally disturbed or sensorially deficient are the most vulnerable to abuse. Like the younger non-verbal child, they are unable to communicate their objectionable experience to responsible adults. Too often they resort to retaliation of a physical nature or to psychological withdrawal.

Whether disabled or normal, the victims of sexual abuse suffer long-term and deep-seated emotional effects that influence their adult relationships for life. Women and men in their forties to sixties emerging from their secret abyss report experiences that continue to haunt them. Each and every victim needs psychological therapy and emotional support. Very disappointing to me is the fact that therapists seem unable to cure the abusers of children—there are no magic drugs or curative psychotherapy. Just as complex as the victim's responses to abuse are the etiologies that drive the perpetrators. It is important to know that child sexual abuse is rarely an impulsive or one-time event—perhaps unlike most date rape—it is premeditated and chronic. The abusers must be stopped, curtailed, closely monitored or removed from society before any more young people are emotionally maimed for life.

CHAPTER 3

THEY'LL NEVER BE ALL RIGHT

PRENATAL ABUSE AND NEGLECT

Prenatal abuse and neglect escalated to notorious heights in the late 1980s, resulting in deplorable infant mortality and morbidity rates for one of the most medically advanced countries in the world. Why? This physician thinks that it was due primarily to the increased prevalence of maternal drug abuse and to teenage pregnancy. Infant morbidity and mortality are largely caused by prematurity. Cases are too often associated with inadequate or non-existent prenatal care for the predictably high-risk pregnancies.

RH-NEGATIVE MOTHERS

The advances of the past twenty-five years have been gratifying to those of us dedicated to the birth of healthy children. With modern prenatal care, most babies do not have to die in utero or suffer brain damage from the affects of Rh-negative blood incompatibilities. The development of the RhoGam vaccine has made the difference.

JENNIFER

Jennifer Smith, born before the preventive vaccine was developed, was not so fortunate. Mrs. Smith, whose blood type was Rh-negative, was about to deliver her third child when her obstetrician alerted me as to the possibility that her baby might have the effects of fetal-maternal blood incompatibility: severe anemia, generalized body edema (swelling) and brain-damaging jaundice. Diagnosis: erythroblastosis fetalis. Thus far, Mrs. Smith's pregnancy had been normal except for an overwhelming fatigue due to caring for her two other children. The spontaneous full-term delivery was uncomplicated. To all lay appearances, the seven-pound baby girl was healthy, and Mr. and Mrs. Smith were delighted to have their first girl.

Within Jennifer's first twelve hours, she developed all the clinical signs of rapidly progressing anemia and jaundice that her cord blood tests had predicted. The feared blood incompatibility between mother and baby was active, causing destruction of her red cells. We knew that if her bilirubin (a breakdown product of red cells causing jaundice) reached a critical blood level of 20 milligrams within twenty-four postnatal hours, irreversible brain damage would result. When Jennifer's bilirubin reached 15 milligrams in a short time, something had to be done immediately. Her condition was deteriorating in other areas as well. An exchange blood transfusion was necessary to replace her dead or dying red cells and reduce her bilirubin. An exchange transfusion was a risky procedure in itself. It required experienced physicians and nurses, special equipment and a standby quality laboratory. In addition to fighting the clock in assembling the above on a holiday weekend, our immediate concern was to stabilize Jennifer in order to give her an optimal chance of surviving the procedure. The factors in her favor were that she was a full-term infant, more rugged than a premature, and that her uncle would donate the fresh, clean compatible blood she needed for her survival. Three hours after we had made the decision to do the exchange transfusion, Jennifer was ready. All systems were go. The entire procedure, taking about two hours, went well and without complications. Now we would have to wait and see if this one transfusion was going to be enough. Only time would ultimately tell us whether or not we had treated her effectively and prevented all the degrees of potential brain damage. As it appeared some fourteen days later, Jennifer seemed to be normal. She was discharged from the hospital. The staff rejoiced almost as much as her parents did as she returned home to her eagerly awaiting brothers.

Today, women identified with having Rh-negative type blood are protected during pregnancy from Rh sensitization by the RhoGam vaccine, which essentially prevents erythroblastosis fetalis (Jennifer's condition described above) in their babies prior to birth. The vaccine is usually given to the prospective mother at twenty-six to twenty-eight weeks of pregnancy and again a few days after delivery of an Rh-positive child.

Whenever an Rh-negative woman experiences any of the following conditions, she should receive RhoGam immediately: miscarriage, induced abortion, serious abdominal injury after thirteen weeks of pregnancy and threatened miscarriage with the continuation of pregnancy.

Subsequent to the development of RhoGam for the prevention of erythroblastosis fetalis, modern medicine has made significant advances in the use of ultrasound and amniocentesis for the early prenatal diagnosis of other birth defects, providing near space-age technology for expectant parents and physicians.

BIRTH DEFECTS

With good prenatal care, babies do not have to be born with underdeveloped brains, paralytic spina bifida or multiple congenital malformations, thanks to fetal-maternal blood screenings, ultrasound and amniocentesis. Current techniques can detect the presence of any number of potentially fatal or disabling malformations in brain, kidney, lung, liver, heart and skeleton very early in pregnancy. Medical advances afford parents and physicians information on the fetus's condition that was previously unavailable. Alpha-feto protein blood tests of the expectant mother have become almost routine in good prenatal care. The latter can detect the presence of a maldeveloped brain, spinal column or Down's syndrome. In the event of a life-threatening defect or one that is untreatable and will severely restrict the quality of life, the informed parent may choose to terminate the pregnancy; other parents may choose to proceed in their preparations for the birth of a disabled child. Sometimes, physicians are able to treat the unborn in utero or immediately after birth. (It is the informed parent's choice as to the child's destiny, not the government's, Civil Liberties Union's, pro-life groups or even the doctor's. The parents alone created the child and they will be responsible for its future for a very long time.) For the majority of parents, learning that their unborn is developing normally through prenatal screening tests is reassuring. Ultrasound pictures are frequently the first bonding of the parents to the fetus, as they see an exciting video of their developing unborn child many months before delivery.

RUBELLA SYNDROME

No longer do babies have to be affected with birth defects as a result of maternal German measles (rubella) infection, thanks to the rubella vaccine. Rubella vaccine given to the nonimmunized woman in advance of conception will protect her unborn. Maternal infection with rubella prior to the sixteenth week of pregnancy causes deafness, cataracts, heart defects, mental retardation or cerebral palsy in her fetus.

SANDRA————————————————————————

Sandra Rubio was to be such a child. Her mother had experienced cold symptoms and a tiny red body rash for a few days during her third month of pregnancy. This mild illness had not required medical attention. Sandra's mother had not mentioned it to the nurse during her next prenatal checkup. The pregnancy went well and Sandra entered the world on her expected birth date. A few minutes later and her parents would have enjoyed the rewards of having a New Year's baby. They could have used the lift. Alex, the father, was a struggling college student and the mother, Betty, a minimum wage earner. Her timing did not detract from their joy over tiny Sandra. While petite at 5½ pounds, she looked and behaved beautifully, eating well and sleeping for six hours at a stretch. The latter behavior was especially appreciated by her dad, whose engineering studies required long periods of intense concentration.

In fact, it wasn't until Sandra was two months old that her physician diagnosed deafness, cataracts, and a pathologic heart murmur. She was also demonstrating a sluggish pattern of physical growth and development. A careful review of prenatal history revealed Betty's fleeting illness. Her brief work in an infant day-care center had evidently exposed her to German measles. Sandra's blood tests and cultures pointed toward rubella as the cause of her problems. The damage to Sandra had occurred when she was a three-month-old developing fetus in her mother's womb. It would last a lifetime. The irony of this covert bug, rubella, creating such an innocuous infection in an adult and doing what it did to Sandra, is incredible. Subtle and treacherous viruses like rubella are not all preventable, but this one was.

HERPES

Unlike rubella, herpes virus, which can be equally damaging to the fetus, has no preventive vaccine. Herpes simplex, commonly known in adults as cold sores, may afflict the unborn or newborn with generalized disease targeting brain, eye and other major organs. This infection in the newborn derives from the mother either through the placenta or in the birth canal. Some prevention of newborn exposure can be accomplished by delivering a woman with genital herpes by cesarean section and bypassing the birth canal.

RICARDO————————————————————

Ricardo Santos, age six months, came to the Birth Defects/ Child Development Clinic upon referral from the city hospital, where he had been born. Mrs. Santos, his mother, with the aid of her neighborhood interpreter, told me the following story. She and her new husband had arrived in the United States from Puerto Rico about ten months before under the sponsorship of a nefarious organization that brought in large groups of young agrarian Puerto Ricans in return for a sizable percentage of their welfare checks. In an attempt to escape this intolerable situation, friends smuggled them to their present location. Her husband was working two jobs: days as a dishwasher and nights as a janitor. When Ricardo was born, mother and child were generally healthy. During her pregnancy, Mrs. Santos noticed a recurrence of small painful blisters on her genitalia, which she had had on and off for years. Unfortunately, these lesions were not present at the time of her two prenatal exams or her precipitous delivery. If the condition had come to medical attention during this time period, Ricardo's problem might have been prevented. (This does not imply that herpes has a cure; treatment modalities have only offered promise of decreasing fetal/infant exposure.)

Ricardo seemed normal at birth with no signs of congenital anomalies or illness. His mother recalled that he was about ten days old when he started to resist breast-feeding and became fussy. Like all first-time mothers, she feared that something was wrong with her milk. During the next two days he became very "dopey" and sluggish. His fitful sleeping was interrupted by shaking spells involving his whole body and he seemed to have a fever. She took Ricardo to the city hospital emergency room (ER) whereupon he was admitted to the hospital with the tentative diagnosis of FUO (fever of unknown origin) and meningitis. Despite multiple test results and nonspecific physical findings, the major clue to his diagnosis was the presence of three small vesicles on his skin. These vesicles, easily overlooked in our haste to treat this critically ill baby, pinpointed the cause of his problem—herpes encephalitis. It was usually fatal. Ricardo would have a better chance of survival than most since we could treat him specifically and immediately rather than giving him an array of antibiotics, of no help in viral diseases but warranted for the delay until the culture results are complete.

Ricardo responded dramatically to the treatment. His mother sat frantically at his bedside for two days and two nights. The critical phase was over, but he would not be rid of herpes nesting in his cells and reactivating the illness periodically. The real questions were: How much harm had it done to his brain and other organs already? How much damage would it do with a recurrence? Careful follow-up throughout childhood with medical, developmental and psychological assessments would be necessary and that was why we, as a multidisciplinary team, were seeing him. The day I saw six-month-old Ricardo, he appeared alert and healthy. Developmentally, he was a bit behind the norm and he had three notable tiny vesicles on his forearm. This made me wonder whether the viral process was continuing elsewhere in the hidden parts of his body. There was no immediate way of telling.

Is it not a perfidious act of nature that both maternal viral infections and drug usage wreak the gravest harms to the developing fetus during the first few weeks after conception, before a woman even suspects that she's pregnant?

FETAL ALCOHOL SYNDROME

One of the most commonly preventable abuses to the unborn is the maternal use of alcohol. For some women even a minimal intake may be damaging. In fact, many experts claim that prenatal exposure to maternal alcohol usage is the single largest cause of mental retardation in young children. The heavier the alcohol intake, the more severely the child will be affected. Present-day warnings are abundant, yet not all women heed them.

GEORGE———————————————————————————

George Sipp, the fifth child of a high-ranking politician and a devoted wife and mother, appeared for evaluation because of slow growth and development. At eighteen months, George measured below the thirty-fifth percentile for height, weight and head size (well under his genetic projections). Something was wrong. He was just beginning to walk with help and had no language at all. In light of these findings, his facial features became even more significant. His upper lip was very thin and smooth; his chin was unusually small; his cheeks were flat; and his eye slits were narrow with prenasal bridge skin folds. Not that George was unattractive; quite the contrary. The untrained eye would see him as an adorable little boy approximately one year old. It was the combination of those facial features, physical growth and developmental lag that led us to the probable diagnosis of "fetal alcohol syndrome." His mother did admit that her social drinking during her husband's election campaign may have gotten out of hand under the pressures of never-ending public appearances. Her older children had been normal even though she had been under the same kind of pressure during those pregnancies. She did say that at age thirty-eight, she was "running out of steam" and hadn't turned down the cocktails and dinner wines that she had abstained from in her earlier pregnancies. She had consoled herself with the knowledge that her pregnant friends had been social drinkers throughout their pregnancies without deleterious effects to their children.

The risk for a mother who drinks, and as a result has a compromised child, is about 40 percent. Fetal alcohol syndrome seems to be dependent upon the individual metabolic manner in which the woman's body handles alcohol. There is no current method of predicting which woman will put her fetus at risk with mild to moderate usage. The across-the-board advice is for all pregnant woman, and those who plan to be, to abstain from any alcoholic beverage. Excess use of cough syrups and sleeping liquids, which tend to have a high alcohol content, should be avoided. Apparently, Mrs. Sipp's friends were lucky; she was not. At no time had she ever thought that social drinking would affect her unborn. Well, it had! Now what?

Because of her history and George's physical findings, the diagnosis of fetal alcohol syndrome was confirmed. While the condition was irreversible and incurable, only George's own maturational progress would reveal how close to normal he would function in the future. Both parents and child needed help. The parents found George's condition and prognosis difficult to accept. As is not unusual for educated, ambitious persons, their degree of disbelief, denial and guilt was significant. Although our primary role as pediatric professionals was to treat the child, parents must be supported, too. A second independent opinion substantiated our diagnosis, facilitating the parents' acceptance. The next step was to assist them in resolving their guilt, and they agreed to counseling with our clinical psychologist. George would be followed by the developmental specialists, who would periodically reassess him. Our instant approach was to enroll him in an early intervention program for children with special needs. One positive outcome of George's problem was that his politician father became an avid sponsor of alcoholic beverage label warnings to pregnant women. His influence and sustained interest in this issue hold out good promise for preventing many children from having fetal alcohol syndrome in the future.

Disheartening is the fact that even today reports pepper the news media of women who drink heavily and knowingly during pregnancy; some up to the onset of labor. Their babies may be born prematurely and some have alcoholic breaths—if and when they breathe at all. More full-blown signs of fetal alcohol syndrome than George developed are joint abnormalities of hands or hips and cardiac defects. In one or two incidents, the parents of an affected child have gone to court to sue the alcohol beverage companies for damages. Whether it is ignorance, lack of appreciation for the life of their unborn child or the insanity of addiction, the fact is that women continue to drink while pregnant. A child born with special needs (or even normal) to an alcoholic mother is unlikely to have a more promising future in childhood than it did in utero. In any case, these babies, like those of drug-addicted mothers, are the victims of a deliberate form of prenatal child abuse that may warrant the most drastic methods of prevention—birth control, temporary sterilization (chemical or surgical) or abortion.

Newborn Drug Addiction

Babies born addicted to drugs are not unique to this generation, just much more common. My first experience with heroin-addicted newborns was at a city hospital on assignment to the delivery room and nursery thirty years ago. In those days, most addicted babies were born to young, uneducated black women, newly arrived from out of state, who literally flocked to Massachusetts for free medical care and high welfare benefits. A seven- or eight-months-pregnant woman getting off a bus and arriving at the city hospital in active labor was not unusual. She would deliver her premature baby and as soon as she could walk, she did, right out the hospital door, leaving the newborn to us. Her compulsion was to avoid the horrors of withdrawal by finding another "fix." (Would that her baby had the same option!)

AHAB

Ahab Jones (named by the staff) was one such infant. He weighed in at four pounds with an Apgar (diagnostic respiratory evaluation) of three, which meant that he was slow to breathe, move and scream. In fact, without intensive resuscitation, he would not have made it. He required assisted respiration for several hours. Once his depressive crisis from narcotic overdose was over, he proceeded to be jittery and irritable with extraordinarily loud, high-pitched, incessant screeching. Subsequently, he had convulsions and high temperatures. Besides treating him supportively for narcotic withdrawal, we had to rule out infection, at least one that we could treat effectively. His mother was gone so we were unable to get a history of what infections or exposures she might have had: strep, staph, venereal diseases, and so on. Does anyone question why pediatrics is often so similar to veterinary medicine in that the respective patients are nonverbal, forcing the doctors to have to rely upon physical examination rather than history for diagnosis?

The invasive procedures necessary to investigate Ahab's possible infections further aggravated his irritable state. It was no fun for him or for us. Several days passed before Ahab improved. A month passed before he started to gain weight. Now that we could look at him less clinically, we saw a handsome, light-brown baby with blue eyes and straight brown hair, with some evidence of mixed parenting. He demonstrated no overt congenital anomalies that might have resulted from his mother's heroin addiction. Developmental delays were still a possibility that only time would reveal. Ahab turned out to be an appropriate nickname for him as we watched him fight back with rage and defy the odds for survival after such a horrible entry into the world. Since his mother never reappeared, she would never know what she was missing by not seeing her child. From a medical standpoint, he seemed perfectly normal, albeit having a slightly small head circumference. The prospects for his ultimate adoption were better than his peers born of similarly drug-addicted mothers. For Ahab, it would be months in foster care before the paperwork and negotiations for placing him with parents would be completed, if at all.

Many drug-addicted mothers, unlike Ahab's, would appear to view their offspring sporadically, but when the time came for the baby's hospital discharge, they were nowhere to be found. Fictitious names, addresses and telephone numbers were commonplace in this population. Still others, equally desperate as those mothers that abandoned their newborns, were doggedly determined to keep them. Their recourse was to seek help through welfare assistance for themselves, their other children and their new baby.

Today, drug usage permeates society at all socioeconomic, racial, age and educational levels. No longer is it confined to the poor, black, young and uneducated women, as it has been in the past. Babies born of drug-addicted mothers today have the added risk of AIDS from intravenous drug usage and multiple sexual encounters.

AIDS BABIES

Acquired immunodeficiency syndrome (AIDS) is the most tragic disease of this century. AIDS in children should be preventable, not to date by vaccine but by cautious, responsible parents. AIDS is caused by a devious and fatal virus, known as HIV (human immunodeficiency virus). Mother-to-child transmission is thought to be the primary route of infection in babies since the advent of screening pretransfusion blood. One study shows that up to 40 percent of babies born to HIV-infected mothers are themselves infected. Pregnant women usually acquire their HIV from intravenous drug usage or HIV-infected sexual partners. During the past five years, AIDS has mushroomed in the adult population to epidemic proportions. The prospect for an increase in pediatric AIDS is probable, as more and more women of reproductive age become infected.

The treachery of HIV infection is the often prolonged leadtime between viral exposure and the individual's measured response in showing HIV-positive blood. More erratic and delayed is the onset of AIDS. In infants born of HIV-positive mothers, identification may take up to fifteen months postnatally before the child's blood tests will accurately reflect whether or not he is infected. The passive transfer of mother's HIV-positive antibodies may persist in the child's blood, masking his own status. For the most part, the transition from HIV exposure to HIV infection to fatal disease is much more accelerated in infants and children than adults. Many die within nine to twelve months after birth.

MEGAN —————————————————————————————

Megan was born to an HIV-positive mother who had apparently been infected by her bisexual husband. Prenatal testing of her mother had alerted us to the chance (30 to 40 percent) that Megan would have a problem. At birth, both mother and child were healthy but HIV-positive. Since the mother was not a drug user, no signs of retarded prenatal growth or congenital anomalies were expected or found. Megan was a beautiful eight-pound baby girl. It could take at least a year or so before we would be able to definitively determine her HIV status, positive or negative, provided that she did not develop symptoms of immunodeficiency in the interim. Those twelve months of joy for other parents, watching their infant develop into a real personality as a toddler, were hell for Megan's folks, not knowing what her fate would be.

Her mother, who so wanted to breast-feed, had to be advised against it since some evidence exists that HIV may be transmitted in breast milk. Despite this, they did enjoy her every progress with delight. Her monthly pediatric checkups documented her good health, growth and development. As expected, the checkups were anxiety-laden for physician and parents alike. The worst thing was watching for signs of AIDS and waiting to know whether Megan would test HIV-positive.

The time (fifteen months) to retest her HIV status finally arrived. Although Megan was still healthy, she tested HIV-positive. How devastating! More watching and waiting. Hoping it might have been a laboratory error, we repeated the test. No luck; it was still HIV-positive. Because Megan had no signs of AIDS, we wanted to believe that she would be one of those positive-to-negative converters or that perhaps we were seeing her mother's lingering antibodies in her blood. Her parents were frantic, simulating the emotions of parents whose child is missing—not knowing if the child is dead or alive, at peace or suffering. Without being able to give them much medical reassurance, we were committed to testing and reexamining Megan as frequently as was prudent until such time as we got some answers. While we could speculate that because both parents as HIV-positive were symptom-free and perhaps just carriers, Megan might not become clinically affected. Her case might be less virulent and respond to anti-AIDS drugs. Our meager knowledge told us otherwise. Nevertheless, we had to deal with the reality of the present. The one positive step we could take was to refer her distressed parents for counseling, which they readily accepted. It was important for Megan, however long she had, to be reared as a normal child without imminent problems. The last time we saw Megan, she was twenty months old, still HIV-positive and overtly well. Troubling was the fact that she was demonstrating a number of nonspecific findings: a falling off of physical growth; an unexpected lag in psychosocial development and hand-to-eye coordination, and a history of several low-grade fever episodes. We never had the opportunity to investigate these findings. Her father obtained a new job and moved the family 1,300 miles away.

JESSE————————————————————————————

Another child born to an HIV-positive mother and in this case a past IV (intravenous) drug user did not fare as well. Jesse, from birth, showed signs of HIV-infection. He was too small for his age; he had an enlarged spleen and liver, poor neurological responses and several other nonspecific signs of illness. Within a week he developed a severe yeast infection involving his mouth, skin and bowel. Intensive treatment was able to rid him of this infection, but his immature and deficient immune system combined with the lack of reserve in his five-pound body could not ward off the next infection. He succumbed to AIDS at age four weeks.

JOSE————————————————————————————

Jose was still another infant born to an HIV-positive mother. She had experienced several vague symptoms suggestive of HIV infection for the previous two years and suspected that she might have had AIDS even before she became pregnant. No testing had been done prior to her fifth month of pregnancy, when she showed up for her first prenatal visit. Later, Jose's mother said that she would have had an abortion had she known in time. Jose entered the world a robust 5½-pound baby boy. His HIV-positive status was not a reliable predictor of his infection since, like Megan, it may have only been reflecting his mother's passively transferred antibodies. For the next three months he and his single mother appeared to be healthy. Then she became ill with a severe pneumonia, requiring hospitalization. Jose was temporarily given over to the care of his aunt. His mother was definitively diagnosed with AIDS. Because of her grave prognosis and the fact that his aunt could not care for him long-term, he was relinquished to the state. Foster care home placement was no easy task since myths of AIDS contagiousness were almost as prevalent among social workers and foster parents as they were among the rest of the population. Jose was finally placed at age five months. During the interim, his pediatric clinic visits revealed that he was growing and developing at a less than optimal rate. That he had been free from serious or prolonged infections was a hopeful sign. He might not go on to develop AIDS despite his lingering HIV-positive testing. In light of his history, slow growth and development could be attributed to maternal deprivation.

At nine months of age, Jose's physical exam was less encouraging. He had enlarged lymph nodes, liver and spleen; his growth rate had dropped significantly; and his previous level of alertness had diminished. The foster mother told us that he had been having almost constant diarrhea for nearly a month that did not respond to treatment. Short-term hospitalization for observation and evaluation was indicated. The tests revealed that, in addition to his persistently HIV-positive blood, he had a compromised immune system. We had to identify Jose as being HIV infected and having AIDS. AIDS, once established in infants, acts much more rapidly than it does in adults. Jose's immediate future was bleak. We had learned that his mother had responded to her treatment for pneumonia and was receiving the drug AZT in a far distant medical center. She had expressed that she no longer wanted to hear about her son, having left him to state responsibility. Since his aunt's whereabouts were unknown, there was apparently no family that gave a damn about the child.

Jose returned to his caring foster mother. Reportedly, he did well for another few weeks, whereupon he came down with an overwhelming infection. Somehow he survived not only our treatment but his infection. At about this time, we were given Federal Drug Administration (FDA) permission to research the administration of AZT to infants. Unfortunately, the state as guardian would not allow any experimentation on its wards. In retrospect, this treatment for AIDS has proven effective in promoting remissions and prolonging life in children as well as in adults. Jose would have neither a remission nor a prolonged life. His future course was characterized by repeated life-threatening infections and nutritional wasting. Rather than the robust newborn and infant we had seen during his first three months, at thirteen months, he held the appearance of a tiny starving child, with haunting eyes and expressionless face. He left us soon afterward to join the others in death from AIDS.

TEENAGE PREGNANCY

The rate of teenage pregnancy in the United States has reached an unprecedented high. It should be a pressing concern to all of us because our children are having children. Teenage pregnancy jeopardizes two generations: the health and education of the mother and the viability and normalcy of the unborn. All forms of child abuse/neglect have a high-risk potential in teenage pregnancy, whether it be prenatal, physical, sexual or psychological. The problems of maternal exposure to drugs or viral or venereal infections are magnified in the adolescent mother. Not only does she forego her natural growing up process—that transition between childhood and adulthood when it's acceptable to have a split personality—but she is forced to confront the realities of adulthood and one of the greatest challenges of life: parenting. Her fantasies abound, yet she inwardly fears a departure from the dependency of childhood. Being a teenager was never easy, no matter what the circumstances in any generation, but today, a child in transition is further confused by her role models: quarreling, divorced or absent parents; amoral, violent musicians and movie idols; dishonest or thieving political and business leaders; and drug-experimenting peers and sexually active friends. It is obvious that the current increase in sexual freedom carries with it many more consequences for the teenage girl than in past generations—many of them potentially fatal to both mother and child.

In the past, those girls that "got into trouble" were a minority. Their options were few and more restrictive: illegal abortion, adoption or support by family with grandmother, aunt or mother raising the child while the teenager went to school or work. "Shotgun marriages" were commonplace. Yes, girls today are still having abortions and in greater numbers, but the abortions are medically safer and government sponsored. Less frequently do girls choose adoption, and their relatives are less willing or able to raise such children. Today, the adolescent single mother keeps her baby with the support of local and federal agencies providing housing, food, clothing, health care and medications. Tragically, emotional and supervisory support for this immature mother and her baby are missing. Concerned public school systems constructively cope with the teenage mother and baby by providing on-site child care and flexible educational schedules to ensure the immediate welfare of both. Such a program was sponsored by Melissa's father as chairman of a suburban school board. Melissa's story follows.

MELISSA

Melissa was a fifteen-year-old tenth-grade student when she became pregnant. She had a long history of emotional disorders. She suffered from obesity up to the age of twelve, when she started a pattern of drastic dieting. However, her dieting result was not as dramatic as she desired, so she self-induced vomiting after eating whatever she craved. (It is called bulimia nervosa and occurs in 20 percent of young women.) Food was not what she craved but peer acceptance. All those years of being ostracized as "fat," combined with her new social awareness of how to be popular with the girls and boys, led her to extreme measures. While binging and purging were making her thin, there were days that she was too weak to carry on her usual activities in school or at home. No one suspected her of purging, not even her parents. Her chronically overweight mother delighted vicariously in her daughter's new image despite the expense of buying her a three-size-smaller wardrobe. For the first time that she could recall, Melissa was getting praise everywhere. The girls at school congratulated her and the boys saw her as an exciting attraction. She was feeling very good about herself as she approached her fourteenth birthday. With social acceptance came the hazards of peer behavior—drugs and sex. Almost everybody that she thought "cool" was doing one or the other, mostly both.

Melissa's initiation occurred at a party one weekend when the host's parents were out of town. It turned into a crash course for this novice. Pot and alcohol were followed by crack-cocaine and ultimately, sexual activities. What a weekend it was for Melissa! Her parents thought she was having good, clean fun on a camping trip with her girlfriend and her parents. Melissa's recollection of this time period was sketchy. It became evident that her intensive introduction to a variety of drugs had laid the grounds for addiction to at least one, cocaine.

Until her allowance was increased so she could buy crack, she got a "lift" from sneaking her parents' alcohol. It took a while for the effects of her newfound habits, drugs and sex, to catch up with her. Her busy, conscientious parents were the last adults to recognize that their darling daughter had problems. Although her mediocre school grades remained the same, her parents were blindly happy with Melissa's metamorphosis. She had friends, social activities and looked like a teenage model.

The identification of her alcohol and cocaine usage came to light just a month before the confirmation of her two-month pregnancy. These combined conditions forecast double jeopardy for her and her fetus. In spite of receiving sex education by her mother and school teachers, Melissa, along with her friends, had thrown caution to the wind during their reckless, drug-induced sexual encounters. The daredevil attitude of the adolescent psyche—"it couldn't happen to me"—and their sense of deliberately planned sex as being "uncool" prevailed.

Melissa's parents, a school board leader and PTA (Parent Teacher Association) leader, withdrew her from school with some personal embarrassment. Somehow, despite a modest income, they found the money to admit her to a residential drug rehabilitation center. A few weeks later her pregnancy was discovered. "What next?" the parents questioned. "How could she hurt herself or us anymore?" Abortion might have been the easy way out except for their conscience. No, they would face up to the situation and try to be supportive. Melissa returned to school but was under house quarantine afternoons, nights and weekends. Her social isolation and her subsequent physical discomfort made her as unhappy as she had ever been. She drifted into a serious depression and withdrew from her folks. With the growing pregnancy, she reverted to early childhoodlike dependency. Psychological counseling did not seem to help. Her parents became more and more convinced that she would be incapable of nurturing and raising her child because of her past and current emotional problems. They had little difficulty in convincing Melissa that adoption would be best for all concerned. Actually, the idea seemed to elevate her mood. Nature was kind in giving her a healthy, normal, seven-pound baby boy, who would easily find adoptive parents.

JULI

Juli was less fortunate. She was a black fourteen-year-old ninth-grader when she became pregnant. A minister's daughter, she was raised in a strict religious household in a semirural community and was a good student. The father of Juli's baby was her first-time lover, whom she had dated for a year with full parental approval. And why not? He was a polite, serious young man of sixteen years from a good family. According to Juli, they had only three lovemaking episodes, each time after church and school functions. Sex had not been discussed at home; it was not approved of as part of the health education program at school. In her naive thinking, she had never entertained the notion that such a pleasurable activity with her best friend would have made her pregnant. Her parents were shocked and angry with the news. What to do? Abortion was out of the question on religious grounds. Marriage was pushed but unacceptable to her boyfriend and his parents, who had college and medical school plans for him. To have the burdens of a wife and child would destroy both. Anger and blame reigned in both his and her families, leaving Juli to bear the child in lonely disgrace. Her folks, especially her mother and the parish women, eventually became supportive. Her father was the last to accept the situation.

Juli continued her studies at school and at home. After delivery, her mother cared for the baby while Juli attended school. The three years to graduation meant a long haul for teenage mother, baby and grandmother, but Juli's parents insisted that she complete high school.

While Juli had always been a healthy child, she developed headaches, edema and high blood pressure (signs of preeclampsia, the gravest form of toxemia in pregnancy) during her seventh month. Preeclampsia would threaten her life and that of her fetus. The initial outpatient treatment was unsuccessful, so she was hospitalized. Intensive medical care did not improve her condition, and signs of fetal distress necessitated an emergency cesarean section. It resulted in a cure for Juli and the live birth of a three-pound baby girl. After weeks and weeks of care in the premature nursery, the baby reached the weight required for hospital discharge. Juli and her mother had visited her almost every day after school. They were so thrilled to bring the fragile two-month-old home.

At this point, Juli wanted desperately to quit school and take full care of her daughter, whom she had named Mary. Her parents would hear none of it. Unlike Melissa, she didn't mind being denied her teenage social life or the after-school activities. She just yearned to be a good mother. When the baby was about a year old, it became obvious that her development was not up to par, even for one who had been born prematurely. The pediatrician diagnosed moderate developmental delays and cerebral palsy for Mary when she was fifteen months old. Special evaluations and therapies would be necessary. The closest disabled children's clinic with the specialists that Mary would require was fifty miles away, creating an extra burden for Juli and her parents. No matter, they would do anything that was needed to help this unfortunate child. Government assistance was forthcoming for the medical expenses, which sky rocketed with braces and other treatments.

The family was coping well until Juli's mother developed cancer. Juli had to drop out of school in order to care for her special-needs baby and her mother. All the plans for Juli's and Mary's future fell apart.

GINGER

Ginger is another adolescent who exemplifies an additional prototype of teenage pregnancy. Ginger came from a single-parent mother, who was chronically on welfare like her own mother and older sister with three children. This white thirteen-year-old seventh-grader had already been sexually active for two years. Her introduction to sexual intercourse happened one night when her seventeen-year-old brother crawled into her bed. Her mother had passed out from drinking and they had finished off her bottle. Soon afterward, she was fair game to her brother's friends, who would bring her presents in exchange for her sexual cooperation. Although she had heard of birth control, she never knew of any other girl her age becoming pregnant. Even after two months of absent periods, the idea that she could be pregnant did not occur to her. Her menstrual periods had always been irregular and seldom did she keep track of them.

After Ginger had visited the health office several times for nausea and vomiting, an astute school nurse questioned her pregnant condition. The nurse's suspicions were medically confirmed. Neither Ginger nor her mother could believe it. Knowing what single parenthood, lack of employment, lack of employable skills and the hopelessness of welfare were like, Ginger's mother and grandmother urged her to have an abortion. Her older sister, with less foresight and two illegitimate children whom she loved, backed Ginger in her determination to carry on with the pregnancy. For Ginger, the pregnancy offered a great excuse to quit school, which she hated, and to "do as she pleased." Being well informed about the welfare benefits to poor mothers and babies, she floated without a care in the world. Ginger looked forward to her own apartment away from her mother's domain where she could have her friends in, party and keep her own hours. It all seemed very attractive to this self-willed child. Little could she comprehend what her future would really be like.

Ginger proceeded in total oblivion with her pregnancy, in marked contrast to her medical caretakers, who were worried about the potential complications of her situation. Her immature body and mind, poor nutritional and health habits, along with her impulsive behavior would stack the deck for her fetus to be born prematurely or possibly have congenital anomalies as a result of her alcohol and crack usage. Her prenatal clinic visits were spotty. No one was able to impress upon her the value of adopting good health habits. This stubborn, shortsighted girl continued to picture her pregnancy as the road to independence—a "playhouse" where she would have her own baby doll to love who would love her back.

She went into a long and difficult labor at thirty-six weeks and delivered a premature four-pound baby boy. Both mother and son cried a lot but did well. Ginger left the hospital sometime before the baby did. She became preoccupied with furnishing her apartment for mother and infant. It was only when the tiny child was handed over to her sole care that she started to realize her grave responsibility. It would not turn out to be the fun and games this thirteen-year-old had envisioned. The baby was always hungry, wet or crying. For an adolescent who had sought the freedom of staying up all night, her infant's round-the-clock demands proved to be gruesome. Her friends and family, living their own lives, pulled away, leaving her a very lonely and isolated young mother. A bit of erratic companionship was available through one of her brother's friends, who had quit school, left home and secretly moved in with her. Perhaps he thought that he was the baby's father. For the most part, he was kind and helpful to Ginger and her baby. At other times, when he was drunk or under the influence of drugs, he punched Ginger around and demanded sex against her wishes (usually called rape). Would her baby be a victim of violence someday? Nobody knows, but the event was not unlikely.

Illicit, illegal drug usage among young people runs rampant across the country. Statistics indicate that children as young as nine years old are using alcohol, marijuana or cocaine products. Uninhibited sexual activity is prevalent among youngsters at an earlier age than ever recognized in US history. The incidence for teenage pregnancy has reached an appalling high with 30,000 girls under age fourteen becoming pregnant each year. About twelve million people a year contract a sexually transmitted disease. Infection with gonorrhea is higher in teenage girls than any other age group and these same youngsters run the risk of permanent infertility later on. The effects of drug usage and sexually transmitted diseases during pregnancy upon the unborn are causing an extraordinary number of babies to be born with birth defects, incurable and irreversible because their brains and nervous systems are damaged.

These newborns "will never be all right." All the medical advances and technology in the world are not going to cure the current social problem of teenage pregnancy or drug- and alcohol-addicted women and their resulting prenatally injured babies.

CHAPTER 4

LOVE BUT LET DIE!

MEDICAL AND PHYSICAL NEGLECT

Neglect is defined as a lack of attention to a child's health needs, which sometimes results in unintentional death. Legal action is seldom taken against the parents or caretaker unless failure to seek medical attention for their child results in morbid injury or death.

The Bill of Rights, contained by the first ten amendments of the United States Constitution, guarantees freedom of religion as proclaimed by the First Amendment. The two outstanding legal restrictions to an individual's right to practice the doctrines of religious faith are polygamous marriage and parents' disobedience of the child labor laws on grounds of religious practice. The latter is assumed to protect the health and safety of children, and yet, an inconsistency seems to exist in federal and state legislative mandates, when followers of certain religions are exempted from public health laws requiring disease-preventive immunizations and from the 1978 and 1984 amendments to the Child Abuse Prevention and Treatment Act of 1974. The amendments state that failure to provide medical care is a form of neglect. Certain children do not receive vaccinations or blood transfusions or lifesaving surgery. The ignorant or poor may not have access to medical care but do not willfully deny curative treatment; others of religious conviction and economic means willfully ignore modern medical treatments for their children. They prefer to rely upon prayers to God for cures and deny the proven medical advances of the last forty-five years.

JOHNNIE

Dr. Niguel, a general practitioner colleague in my neighborhood, was called one morning at 2:00 A.M. to see Johnnie because he was not breathing. When he arrived, this three-year-old child was blue and moribund. His parents sobbed out that he had had a high fever, a sore throat, an inability to drink and delirium for several days. Before doing an emergency tracheotomy to provide air to his small lungs, the physician noted a gray, tenacious membrane coating the entire back of Johnnie's red, raw throat. The air-obstructing membrane turned out to be extensive, reaching into his trachea. This deadly membrane is unique to a disease that was all but eradicated in the United States by the 1950s. In fact, it is so rarely seen that most physicians would never have recognized it. Diphtheria was the culprit—preventable by vaccine and curable by antitoxin and antibiotics. Sure enough, Johnnie had not been immunized since his parents did not believe in it. The lifesaving measures taken by Dr. Niguel were unsuccessful in reviving the child. The disease process had gone too far as he slipped beyond a return to life. (Of all the deaths a physician faces, the ones caused by a preventable or curable disease are the toughest to take.)

CRAIG ————————————————————————————

Craig was a healthy little boy born to loving parents of strong religious faith. His father was a young, intelligent, aspiring writer for a top-notch newspaper; his mother had had a career as a legal aide prior to Craig's birth. She delighted in caring for him. His growth, development and bright, affable nature would have made any parent proud. Unlike many children who reach the age of two years, he had never had an injury or a day of illness.

The day came when Craig was abruptly less interested in eating and seemed to have a "tummy ache." Increasingly, he became more uncomfortable. All the signs of a bowel obstruction developed. His sensitive parents knew that he was seriously ill when his condition worsened despite their nursing care. They devoutly relied upon their faith to cure Craig. For five days, they prayed intensively for his recovery while lovingly caring for him. Meanwhile, their only child screamed intermittently with pain, refused to take food or drink and grew weaker. Ultimately, he lapsed into a coma; then, the relief of death. Craig's parents' "steel faith" in the curative powers of their religion never wavered despite their ordeal of watching him suffer and slip away. One might assume that their faith was stronger than Johnnie's parents', who did call for medical help, albeit at the end of his life.

Craig's parents were found guilty of manslaughter by a jury. The right to religious freedom that is guaranteed by the First Amendment was not challenged, but rather the child's right to conventional medical treatment that could have saved his life. (The local court carefully avoided the constitutional question that is the sole province of the US Supreme Court and may be addressed in the future.)

The reason Johnnie's parents were never charged with his death is unknown. Perhaps in 1960, in the small town where he lived and died, the medical examiner failed to alert the district attorney of the circumstances, or perhaps the district attorney elected not to touch the issue of parental religious rights versus a child's right for survival. National legislative attention toward child abuse and neglect was just emerging in the 1960s, after C. Henry Kempe, MD, in 1961 reported medical evidence of the battered child syndrome before the annual meeting of the American Academy of Pediatrics. Only recently have professionals, governmental leaders and the public acknowledged the more subtle forms of child abuse and neglect.

PHYSICAL NEGLECT

The last report in 1986 by the US Department of Health and Human Services indicates that of the three categories of child neglect (physical, educational and emotional), physical neglect is by far the most frequent. In their data collection, almost 600,000 children were identified.

Within the seven recognized forms of physical neglect are:

REFUSAL OF HEALTH CARE: Failure to provide or allow needed care in accord with recommendations of a competent health care professional for physical injury, illness, medical condition or impairment; and

DELAY IN HEALTH CARE: Failure to seek timely and appropriate medical care for a serious health problem which any reasonable layman would have recognized as needing medical attention.

Two additional forms of neglect pertaining to health are specified under different subcategories:

OTHER PHYSICAL NEGLECT: inadequate nutrition, clothing or hygiene; and

GENERAL OR UNSPECIFIED NEGLECT: lack of preventive health care. (The former excludes cases of children whose parents are financially unable to provide proper nutrition, clothing, hygiene or a safe living environment.)

Since neglect is attributed with causing more child fatalities than is abuse, early intervention becomes even more critical.

DANIEL

Ten-month-old Daniel was accidentally discovered to be a victim of nutritional neglect when his mother brought him to the office of a private physician after he had suffered two days of high fever. Physical examination easily diagnosed an acute ear infection as the cause, but a more serious condition was inadvertently diagnosed by the blood tests: iron and vitamin B-12 deficient anemia and protein deficiency. In-depth history revealed that Daniel was the firstborn child to parents who adhered to a strict vegetarian diet known as "Vegan." Vegan diets are completely devoid of any animal products. At times of high biological needs (such as pregnancy, lactation and infancy) for vitamins, iron, minerals and protein, Vegan, without supplements, falls short. This extreme vegetarian diet puts the mother and infant in jeopardy. For whatever reasons—ignorance or willful noncompliance with professional health advice—Daniel's mother never took vitamins, iron or mineral supplements pre- or postnatally. She breast-fed her baby. Later, she fed Daniel small amounts of pureed Vegan diet, which she and her husband consumed.

Not all vegetarian diets necessarily compromise the nutrient needs and growth of infants and children. The lacto-ovo diet permits the eating of eggs, milk products and vitamin and mineral supplements but prohibits red meat, poultry, seafood and fish. The semivegetarian diet allows poultry, seafood and fish intake and prohibits only red meats. Either of the latter two diets, because of greater flexibility in providing more choices, are able to satisfy the special physiological needs of pregnant and lactating women and of their infants and children if menus are planned to meet the extra requirements. Contrasted to the Vegans, other vegetarians are usually receptive to modern medical science and conventional medical treatments. (Prophylactic immunizations and periodic baby checkups were contrary to Daniel's parents' belief and consequently not pursued.) Until recently, it was rare to see a baby of Daniel's parentage (white, middle class and educated) with nutritional deficiencies. Perhaps with warnings that animal protein and fat consumption are correlated with cholesterol-based heart and artery diseases, our health-conscious society has created an overkill for persons who gravitate toward absolutes; all or nothing, or, if a little is good, more is better. The rapidly growing infant and young child has very specific nutritional demands, different from the adult and crucial to the normal maturation of the blood, bone, muscle, brain and neurological system. The resultant damage from untreated malnutrition is often irreversible. (It includes rickets, bowed limbs, retarded growth, skin, hair and eye problems and, for the severely protein deficient, brain damage.) These conditions are usually seen in poor, famine-stricken, underdeveloped countries. A projection is that the United States will see more nutritionally deprived infants as the popularity for pure vegetarian diets increases.

The particular problems with Vegan diets focus on insufficiencies of protein, calories, vitamin D, vitamin B-12 and iron. Daniel's condition exemplified all of the above in one degree or another. Treatment of his anemia and multiple-complex problems warranted hospitalization. His parents' antagonism toward western medical diagnosis and care was difficult to overcome, but it was— more out of their love for Daniel than any change in their belief. Daniel was admitted to the hospital, where further diagnostic tests and x-rays identified vitamin D deficiency with early rickets. The treatments to correct the anemia and the vitamin D deficiency were simple; the initial response was dramatic. A long-term therapeutic victory would only be realized if the parents would comply with a nutritional change consistent with his physiological needs throughout early childhood.

PAUL————————————————————————————

The emergency medical technicians (EMTs) brought Paul to the ER after he was hit by a car while riding his bike. This ten-year-old was seriously injured with trauma to his head, limbs and abdomen. Before the tests, exam and x-rays were completed or his shock was fully stabilized, his parents arrived. The surgeons explained his critical condition: fractured arm and leg, head contusions and probable tears of his liver and spleen, judging by the significant amount of blood within his abdomen. Emergency surgery was imperative to save his life, and blood transfusion was a vital part of that process. Paul's parents readily gave permission for the surgery and anesthesia but absolutely refused permission for any blood transfusions. Despite the efforts of the surgeons to convince them that no nonblood substitutes could provide the oxygen-carrying ability of real blood to replace Paul's massive loss, they would not budge from this doctrine of their religious faith. Reluctantly, the surgeons, having no option, had to operate in order to stop the bleeding. They knew that the boy's risks were multiplied without benefit of blood replacement. Time was critical. Paul's condition was worsening. The hospital administrator set the process in motion for a court order to permit lifesaving blood transfusions for Paul, overriding his parents' decision. At the operating table, the surgeons discovered what they had expected—an abdominal cavity full of blood trickling from lacerations of the liver and spleen. The spleen was tied off and removed, thus stopping that source of hemorrhage. The liver was repaired. Paul's vital signs were erratic throughout the operation. He failed to stabilize even after the bleeding was stopped. His hemoglobin was dangerously low. Improvement was unlikely without transfusion. The on-call judge had not been located by the time Paul was transferred from the operating room (OR) to the intensive care unit (ICU). His fractures would have to wait for repair until his grave condition had improved since he was simply unable to withstand more surgery. Also waiting was the typed and cross-matched blood, which he would receive as soon as permission was granted. Paul faded away when he experienced an intractable drop in blood pressure and his heart stopped. Ironically, the court permission came less than twenty minutes later.

UNNAMED CHILD

Barbara and Mike were nearing their nine-and-one-half-month wait for the birth of a second child. All was ready for the home delivery, which the midwife assured them would be normal, easy and uncomplicated. Barbara awakened at 2:00 A.M. when her water broke, flooding the bed. The initial frequency of her labor pains predicted a relatively rapid process. Eight hours later, she still had not delivered and everyone was nervous, thinking that something must be wrong. Her first labor and delivery at home had been short and easy. Mike and the midwife assured the exhausted, frightened mother-to-be with prayer, which seemed to soothe her. She dropped off into a well-needed, brief, but troubled sleep whenever the pain lulled. No one seemed to notice that Barbara was quietly going into shock. When red blood trickled out from her vagina and her color bleached, the midwife, over Mike's objections, demanded her emergency transfer to the local hospital. Upon arrival, the medical assessment confirmed that she was hemorrhaging. Blood replacement was imperative in order to save her life and, if not too late, that of the baby. Mike's and Barbara's religious faith prohibited blood transfusions. Mike refused permission for his semiconscious wife but would allow transfusion of a nonblood fluid to combat the shock. (This alone was a compromise for a believer—but not good enough. There is no substitute for the oxygen-carrying power of red blood cells.) An IV fluid was pumped into Barbara to counteract her worsening shock. The doctors were losing her, but they still thought they might be able to save her baby. Mike gave his consent for an emergency cesarean section to retrieve the child and to stop his wife's bleeding. Too late! The baby had died and the mother was lost as well.

MARK————————————————————————————

Tetanus infection is still a killer of those persons who are not immunized or promptly treated with tetanus immune globulin (TIG), tetanus antitoxin (TAT), and antibiotics. Mark, age six, was growing up with his seven brothers and sisters on a small, self-supporting farm in the Midwest, when he developed a sardonic grin. It was in marked contrast to his usual open, wide-lipped, happy smile. Other signs of tetanus infection—a stiff neck and difficulty swallowing (first his solid foods and then liquids and his saliva)—followed. Within three days of the onset, his parents observed intermittent twitching of various parts of Mark's body. Their second son had always been a healthy and happy-go-lucky child, their best eater, the most active and robust, and, definitely, their most dedicated little farm helper with the animals. About a week or so earlier he had stepped on a rusty nail in the pigpen and had sustained a deep puncture that festered for a while and then seemed to heal over. His parents did not believe in modern medicine, preferring to rely upon their faith to cure any bodily ills. Their children had never been immunized or seen a medical doctor or nurse. Even when Mark's older sister lay semiconscious in bed for a week after a bout of measles that all the other kids had endured without incident, his parents' faith never wavered. They stood fast, never calling in medical help. Although she recovered from her measles encephalitis, the residual neurological damage was significant. This nine-year-old was left with paralysis of the right side of her body, impairing speech, manual dexterity and walking.

It was a surprise to Mark's parents that he was having such trouble since he had always been the stronger and healthier of all their children. Every time the others got some childhood illness, be it chicken pox, mumps, whooping cough or the common cold, Mark had the mildest case and was the quickest to recover. His continued inability to eat or drink, combined with the progressively intense and painful spasms involving his arms and legs, now lasted several minutes. It frightened everybody. Around-the-clock prayers were his parents' solution and salvation. After ten days of watching Mark suffer, become weaker and weaker and lose bladder and bowel control, his uncle (a nonbeliever) threatened the parents that if they would not take their son to the hospital, he would. They thought about it long and hard all night, searching their souls and questioning themselves as to why their faith was not strong enough for their prayers to heal Mark. The next morning, still undecided about letting Mark be treated by conventional medicine, the decision was forced by Mark's new alarming episode: a prolonged spasm of the larynx, which made him turn blue with respiratory obstruction. It passed and they hurriedly loaded Mark into the back seat of their old station wagon. With his mom at his side comforting him, Mark's father anxiously started off on the eighty-mile distance to the hospital. The trip was difficult since the sounds from the road's heavy trucks roaring and tooting and the sunlight flashing through the windows triggered Mark's spasms, which became almost constant. Less than twenty miles from the hospital, Mark had another laryngeal spasm, which lasted long enough to be fatal.

LAURA————————————————————————

The survival of a child with insulin-dependent diabetes (IDD) demands medically oriented treatments. About 0.2 percent of American children can be expected to have IDD. Of these children, some are the offspring of parents devoted to certain Christian religious sects that don't believe in modern medical science. These children, denied insulin and treatment of their chemical imbalance crises, will die.

Laura, a previously chubby eight-year-old, experienced a drastic loss of weight during the past two months despite her ravenous appetite and craving for soft drinks. Most disturbing to her and her parents was the fact that she had started to wet her bed and was less energetic than she had been. On the other hand, they were happy to see her slimming down while still being a good eater. They really didn't think anything was wrong. An annual routine urinary screening test at school to detect "silent" urinary tract infections in girls revealed that Laura had large amounts of glucose in her urine. The school nurse contacted her parents, recommending that Laura be seen by her family doctor (little knowing that she had none). A second call, this time from the school physician, prompted the parents to take Laura's abnormal urine test more seriously. Their concern over Laura's progressive weight loss, physical and mental inactivity and persistent bed-wetting stimulated them to act. Being intelligent people, they first read what medical books they could find in the local library (all out of date and misleading); next, they discussed with members of their family the possibility of seeking medical attention; and lastly, they deliberated as to which course they should pursue for their daughter. Breaking a covenant by resorting to medical diagnosis and treatment was a serious matter. Their ultimate decision was to have Laura evaluated by a holistic physician. It turned out to be a good compromise since medicine and faith should be complementary, not antagonistic or exclusive of one another. ("Old school" physicians knew this. How many hopeless cancer patients who had exhausted all treatments available in medicine have turned their disease around by believing or developing a positive attitude? Going through this life is not always easy and most rational people understand that body, mind and soul need all the help they can get.)

The physician confirmed a diagnosis of IDD. This is a serious disease that lasts a lifetime and requires careful balancing of insulin with dietary intake and metabolic demands. The management of diabetes in children is a very tricky job for a number of reasons: the daily insulin requirements are apt to fluctuate widely, reflecting the varying metabolic demands driven by exercise, growth requirement and dietary intake. The child's psychosocial adjustment is also different from his or her peers, while the fear of having a potentially fatal illness is added to the ordinary stress of growing up. The patient and the family must both be involved in compliance to the medical regimen. The optimal approach is provided by a multidisciplinary team, including an experienced pediatrician, a dietitian and a psychologist. Laura's new physician, while not an expert in childhood diabetes, was an excellent choice for this family: he listened to their philosophy that a strong faith in God would heal all bodily ailments (mind and soul over matter). The doctor was sophisticated enough to convince her parents that Laura's illness would need a combination of both medicine and faith. If her diabetes were medically treated, her most troublesome symptoms of extreme weight loss, listlessness and bed-wetting would be eliminated. At the same time, their belief in self-healing would promote Laura's confidence in her self-will as a controlling force in her well-being. With some reluctance, her parents agreed to the medical management plan: daily insulin injections, blood and urine testing for regulation of insulin dosage, strict dietary control and educative diabetes counseling for Laura and her parents. It would be a very foreign pattern for people who had never been dependent upon medical direction but absolutely necessary for the maintenance of their daughter's health. There would be no miracles and they would endure lots of pitfalls in her future course.

Over the subsequent weeks, Laura and her parents complied reasonably well with her physician's management program. Her physical and mental inertia disappeared, and she stopped losing weight and wetting her bed. Best of all, she didn't mind being a special person—with all the attention she was getting from her parents, the school teacher and her friends. The truth of the matter was that her parents, who loved her dearly, *did* mind breaking their religious covenant. As is the case with many folks on maintenance medication, once the symptoms subside and they are feeling better, they discontinue the medication, thinking they don't need it anymore. While some adults may not show any immediate effects, this is not true for children with diabetes. Lack of insulin will produce conditions that jeopardize their very lives. Apparently, the physician's message to Laura's parents did not take hold or they thought the medicine had boosted her to the point where faith could take over. Not so. Within a day her untreated diabetes took over, causing her to develop the serious complication of ketoacidosis (mental confusion, nausea, vomiting, dehydration and weight loss due to faulty carbohydrate metabolism). Her persistent vomiting and abdominal pain led her medically naive parents to think of food poisoning, with which they were familiar. They nursed her and waited for it to subside. It wasn't until she lapsed into a coma that they considered her condition to be serious and perhaps related to her diabetes. They resumed her insulin dosage but with no response from Laura. Being unable to reach her doctor by phone, in desperation they transported her to the local hospital ER. Upon their arrival, the admitting physician officiously diagnosed Laura's condition (ketoacidosis) and started an IV against their protest. The nurse scolded them for not giving her the insulin that she required. Before they had a chance to finish their argument about the IV, they were confronted with a bunch of papers, including questions about personal history and financial status to be answered. An ER assistant reviewed the papers with them while Laura was still lying there, unconscious. The callous manner in which things were being done was a far cry from their previous experience in the physician's office. They were so angry and offended that if Laura were not in such poor shape, and if they could have reached her doctor, they would have scooped her up and left. (Remember that these folks were completely unfamiliar with the usual medical process. They feared losing control more than most of us.) The next step, admitting the child to the hospital, was just that—losing control, but they could hardly fight it in light of Laura's condition. Their fears were somewhat allayed as they reached the pediatric floor, with its colorful, homey decor and friendly staff. How marked the contrast to the stark, white-tiled ER rooms, loaded with mechanical devices, medical paraphernalia and horribly militaristic personnel. When they learned they could stay at Laura's bedside, they felt even better. Their daughter woke up at about the same time her doctor arrived. He explained what had happened to Laura and, in an unaccusing way, stressed her daily lifetime need for insulin. Fully cognizant of Laura's close call, the parents promised to be cooperative in her management. The years ahead would see other diabetic crises for Laura, provoked by febrile (elevated body temperature) illnesses, physical or emotional stresses, teenage rebellion and pregnancy, but, on the whole, compliance to her treatment program was good. Several potential crises were probably aborted by prompt intervention.

How many children with loving, economically secure parents, who are exclusively committed to spiritual healing or faith healing, will suffer, be disabled or die as a result of their parents refusing them medical treatment? Admittedly, as a physician, I am biased toward healing and preventing disease and death, with all that scientific medicine has to offer, in unison with psychological and philosophical support—from religious beliefs or other sources. Few experienced medical practitioners would dispute the powerful effects of faith in the healing process nor would they guarantee that drugs, surgery or irradiation alone will cure everybody. The growing numbers of adult patients with psychosomatic illnesses outweigh the number of patients with organic illness in most any medical office these days. A strong belief in "mind over matter" or some power higher than man may provide them with the best cure of all. Within the pediatric age group, psychosomatic symptomatology is unusual. Parents—whether believers in conventional medicine or believers in religious healing—should become acquainted with the signs of serious illness in children that require immediate medical attention before taking a "wait and see" or prayer approach. More kids might be helped or even saved if spiritual or faith healers with sick children would give them the benefit of a medical assessment in order to determine the diagnosis and treatment options. Then they can weigh the information intelligently in terms of the child's best interests before opting for the exclusion of medical treatment.

Up to this day, a person's constitutional right to freedom of religion is zealously preserved, and that is part of our American heritage. The question bottoms out in terms of children: Does the parent have the right to refuse the child proven medical, often lifesaving cures that would promote their health and well-being?

It is the question that was addressed by the Massachusetts Supreme Judicial Court in 1991 in the McCauley case. An eight-year-old diagnosed with leukemia needed blood transfusions, which his parents refused on religious grounds. In making their deliberation, the court weighed four interests: the natural rights of the parents, the interests of the child, the interests of the state in preserving life, and the ethical integrity of the medical profession. They ruled that the interests of the child and the state's interest in preserving life took priority over the parents' right to refuse medical treatment. The court further stated that parental rights "do not clothe parents with life and death authority over their children." Interesting to note is the fact that the US Supreme Court has avoided taking up the freedom of religion matter.

CHAPTER 5

WHOSE BUSINESS IS IT?

PHYSICAL ABUSE

Physical abuse of children seldom comes to media or public attention unless it results in death. Yet children throughout the country suffer daily from beatings, burns, slashing, chaining and physical abuse of all sorts and degrees. This is taking place in the 1990s, at a time when corporal punishment of adults, even the most vicious criminals, is not acceptable to the majority of society. The dual standard may stem from the confusion by parents and others about the difference between discipline and punishment. The debated rights and responsibilities of parents to rear their children in whatever way they see fit, morally and legally, conflict with society's obligation to protect and intervene on the behalf of abused children. Physical punishment ideology has survived since Victorian times, when it was a major method of discipline for an offending person, especially a vulnerable child. This way of thinking wasn't popularly questioned until Sigmund Freud illustrated in his early studies that the punisher was reacting to his own subconscious repressions and anxieties (guilt-punishment theory). Accepting this theory, sensitive parents pulled away from the idea that physical punishment of their children was integral to proper child rearing. Others went behind closed doors, as they continue to do more than a century later.

Granted, there are some seemingly incorrigible children, constantly crying or ailing; the incompetent and noncompliant, mentally retarded or physically handicapped; or the just plain obstinate, who try the patience of the most self-controlled adult. These children are the most vulnerable to the "learned" violent responses of their parents. Many lines separate discipline from punishment, but basically, the latter exceeds the purpose of sheer discipline to correct and extends to uncontrolled morbid injury. Thus, when I saw a small child whacked across the supermarket aisle by her frantic mother, I didn't know what to do: pick up the crying child to comfort her, verbally lash out at the outrageous mother or report the incident to some absent authority. I wanted to do all three. My greatest fear was that if the child was slapped around in public, what must be happening to her in the privacy of her home? However, like most people, I did nothing. I became one of the majority of concerned but incompetent observers who witness this despicable behavior.

AMY

As a pediatric intern more than thirty years ago in Boston, I became acquainted with my first abused child. Amy, a two-year-old, was admitted to the ER. She was blue, unconscious and not breathing. Resuscitation was successful, and although still unconscious, her vital signs were good. Her frightened young mother told us that she had found Amy drowning in the bathtub. The black emergency police wagon had transported them to the hospital.

(Equipped ambulances, EMTs or laypersons with CPR [cardiopulmonary resuscitation] training were not available in those days.)

It was about midnight when this blue-eyed, blond-haired, tiny girl on a stretcher arrived on my pediatric floor. The senior nurse on duty recognized her immediately. Amy had been a patient for three months the year before. At that time, she had been admitted for "failure to thrive," cause unknown. Diagnostic tests had ruled out organic diseases, so the medical conclusion for this well-developed but undersized, pale, irritable baby was malnutrition. (Usually it was caused by maternal deprivation due to ignorance or neglect.) The nurse recalled that after weeks and weeks of nurturing and tender, loving care by the nurses, the child had thrived both physically and socially. Amy's mother, Nina, had visited her two or three times at the beginning of her hospital stay and just prior to discharge. Because of the above circumstances, hospital and community social workers and public health nurses were solicited to assist Amy's mother in child care. They could provide ongoing support for parenting upon her return home. The senior nurse couldn't tell me what had happened to Amy after her departure from the hospital months ago, whether Amy's mother was unavailable or disinterested in the professional community's offers of help, or whether the support system with its various agencies had failed. What I did know was that Amy was back in nine months later with a near-death experience.

Examination showed Amy to be a too-small-for-age, thin, comatose white female. There were multiple black, blue and yellow bruises on her otherwise pale skin. In fact, a few of these marks resembled adult finger imprints. She was breathing without assistance. Other than an IV sugar/saline drip line and urine collection bag, she required no intrusive medical paraphernalia. Her neurological reflexes were good, perhaps indicating a good prognosis, given the severity of her drowning insult. (A physician's gravest concern in such cases is irreversible brain damage.) Ever so slowly during the next days this comatose child showed signs of recovery: a twitch here and a cry there whenever staff stimulated her for hygienic, feeding or exam purposes. When she opened her eyes and responded to the sights and sounds around her, we knew that the IV could be removed and she could take nourishment by mouth.

Now fully conscious, it was apparent that Amy possessed a greater apprehension of people around her, especially of men, than the usual hospitalized child of her age. Her haunting stares, unprovoked defenses against any touching or cuddling, reluctance toward receiving a toy or stuffed animal and, primarily, her cowering posture suggested to us a child distrustful of people. While she would hesitantly reach for "mommy" (Nina, on her infrequent visits), Amy never did cling to her, cry or have difficulty separating when the visits were over. Given the circumstances of Amy's two hospital admissions, her diagnoses and her social-emotional behavior, this child appeared to be the victim of physical abuse as well as nutritional and psychological neglect.

From what Nina had told us individually, the social worker and I were able to put together a history of Amy's short life. After graduating from high school, Nina had worked as a file clerk and lived at home with her hardworking, Roman Catholic parents. She had been going steady with "Joe" for two years. He was described as a twenty-year-old, striving apprentice plumber. Nina was nineteen when Amy was conceived. Neither Joe nor her parents took her pregnancy lightly. Joe did not dispute his forthcoming fatherhood but wanted Nina to terminate the pregnancy. (Legal abortion was not an option in 1958.) Both of her parents, having strong religious convictions, were highly critical of Nina for having premarital sex. For them, the only solution to her problem was to marry Joe. Although they used every means possible to compel them to marry, Joe would not concede to their demands. Consequently, Nina was forbidden to see Joe. Despite their love for each other, it was no longer possible to carry on with any kind of a relationship under such parental threats. Joe was scared off for good.

As her pregnancy advanced and she grew larger and larger, her parents' animosity toward her for making a "mistake" made Nina's home life miserable. In addition, her morning sickness never subsided. Because she was taking too much sick time, she lost her job and medical benefits when she was six months along. Eventually, Nina was processed by the appropriate welfare agency for medical assistance. Her meager unemployment compensation fell far short of buying maternity clothes or paying full board to her parents. The long-awaited day came on schedule. She delivered a beautiful, seven-pound baby girl.

Things had gone well for the first few months of Amy's life, with doting grandparents and teenage aunts and uncles who adored her every waking hour. If anything, she may have been overstimulated. This changed, however, when Nina started to date again. Amy was left in her grandmother's care a bit too often for this tired, hardworking woman. Nina's father didn't like her new boyfriend or Nina's late hours. The end result was that everybody fought. Nina and Amy moved out.

A new phase in Nina's and Amy's life was about to begin. "Bill," the new boyfriend, found an apartment for the three of them. Her parents objected vehemently to this live-in arrangement without marriage. After all, Nina already had one illegitimate child. Not seeing their first grandchild, who, legitimate or not, they had come to love, added fuel to their anger. They disowned Nina. Now Nina had lost a very valuable source of family support for herself and Amy. Bill was considered a "good guy," except for his occasional loss of temper. He demonstrated his love for them by helping out with the rent, food and Amy's care. Nina was able to work part-time because Bill was home a lot since it was winter and he was between construction jobs. As is not unusual for a baby, Amy got sick with a high fever. She cried constantly and refused her bottle. Nina took her to the outpatient clinic, where she received a prescription for her throat and ear infection. Getting the needed medication into an infant who refuses her bottle, or even to open her mouth, was a further challenge for this inexperienced mother. Finally, Amy recovered from her illness, but she never regained her weight loss or ceased to be fussy. According to Nina, this was the reason for her first Boston City Hospital admission at twelve months for "failure to thrive." During this three-month hospital stay, Amy picked up significantly in her growth. Social service, having no reason to object to her discharge, agreed to it, as did the medical staff, and Nina eagerly took her healthy baby home.

Once again, in her current hospitalization after near-drowning, Amy was making remarkable progress. However, it was apparent that she was moderately behind the two-year-old age group expectation in verbal and social development. (Verbal and social skills are particularly dependent upon environmental caretaker stimulation.) Since Nina was not anxious to take Amy home right away because of some trouble with Bill and her job, the staff thought it best to keep her in the hospital as a boarder. It was not uncommon to retain a child for nonmedical purposes until parental or other placement was ready.

In this case, the question of child abuse and neglect antecedent to her admission was very much on our minds. Given the finger imprint bruises, the lack of details surrounding her so-called bathtub drowning, her delayed social and verbal development without findings of mental retardation or autism, and especially her peculiar responses to her mother, we were obligated to consider physical and emotional neglect as a very real possibility. Perhaps we were even dealing with a failed homicide. No matter what the causes for Amy's condition, we all felt relieved that her postponed discharge would give social service and the child protective agencies time to investigate our suspicions. More importantly, Amy would be in a safe place for a little while longer. After almost a month, the investigation into Amy's home life was still incomplete.

Nina, having resolved her differences with Bill, insisted upon taking her daughter home. We had no grounds upon which to further delay Amy's discharge, so she left us.

It was several months after I moved on from the city hospital that I read in the newspaper about a child matching Amy's description and first name as "Reported Missing." I never saw a follow-up of the outcome. I presume that Amy is still missing or dead. The delegated agencies never did determine who was responsible for her bruises or her near-drowning: the mother, Bill, or both. Collectively, we were all responsible: Joe, her biological father, who didn't want his baby; her grandparents, who disowned their daughter and grandchild; and the hospital staff and the local and state agencies, whose essential purpose for existence is to protect children from harm. After so many years of seeing abused infants and children, the memory of this first child continues to haunt me.

PHILLIP AND JOEY————————————————————————

Two children with whom I became acquainted had suffered intentional trauma to their feet, which my colleagues and I had to conclude was the result of physical abuse. Phillip, age seven, showed up on the first day of school walking in a very stilted manner, grimacing in pain. A teacher who had known him the previous year suspected something was hurting him. She asked him what was wrong and he became very defensive, refusing to answer her questions. When she took Phillip to the school nurse, he just broke down in tears. Removal of his ragged sneakers and hole-filled socks revealed the cause of his faulty gait: both feet were discolored, blue to yellow, and swollen to the point where his toes could not be separated. The medical impression was that his soles had been caned with a hard object. It was probable that a number of small bones had been fractured. Phillip's parents were contacted about the findings and offered no plausible reason for his problem, saying that they and their son had been camping and mountain climbing over the Labor Day vacation and Phillip had probably injured his feet at that time. Child abuse was a more plausible cause. The child protection agency was notified. In the meantime, the child needed to be more thoroughly examined and x-rayed in order to verify the extent of his injuries and to receive appropriate treatment. The latter would have to be at the discretion of his parents. Keeping him off his feet and from walking around school in pain was definitely indicated. Despite our reluctance to send him home, he had to be dismissed from school. Worrisome on our part was the possibility that he would not receive treatment and might be even further abused by his parents before the state child protective agency could intervene.

Joey, age six, was the other child with foot trauma who came to our attention. Joey returned to school after a Christmas recess and was observed walking painfully. Upon examination, he had what appeared to be cigarette burns on his feet and buttocks. Joey had several other problems: hyperkinesis (learning and behavioral disfunction), mental retardation, seizures and erratic bladder and bowel control. Because of the greater demands on parents and caretakers presented by handicapped children, they are in a high-risk group for neglect and abuse. In Joey's case, it was learned that he was the youngest of three siblings; the two older children had been reported by schoolteachers and neighbors as possible abuse victims to the child protective authorities. It was also known that the parents were illegal drug users. The investigative social worker had visited on a day when everything looked okay. The result was that the child abuse complaint was deposited in a nonactive file and the social worker went on to a more pressing case. Maybe it was because Joey was handicapped and the evidence of burns irrefutably intentional that his child abuse complaint was more promptly investigated than Phillip's. All three children were subsequently placed in foster care until the parents could be rehabilitated. His non-handicapped siblings were ultimately returned to their parents. Joey was not. He was considered to have special needs beyond the coping skills of his parents. Although he would be deprived of nurturing by his biological parents, his ever-increasing needs would be met by a team of trained persons whose own problems would not overshadow his care and best interests.

MARTY

It was about midnight in the pediatric emergency room when a five-month-old baby arrived in critical condition. He was comatose and breathing irregularly; his color was poor and one pupil was larger than the other (usually indicating brain involvement). X-rays showed a skull fracture, questionably dislocated cervical vertebrae, fractures of the left arm and leg, in addition to healing fractures of his ribs. The child expired on the examining table. We could not revive him. His mother's boyfriend, who brought him in, told us that Marty had fallen off a table while he was changing his diaper and had momentarily turned away to answer the phone. He had been baby-sitting, as he often did on those nights when the baby's mother was working. His story was plausible, but was the fall accidental? We thought not, in light of the findings. Our responsibility was to sort out the medical evidence versus his story. On physical examination, the child was well-developed, well-nourished and without superficial signs of abuse. Finding healing rib fractures with x-rays, along with the boyfriend's glassy eyes and the smell of alcohol on his breath, added to our suspicions. The fractured ribs could be evidence of previous squeezing of the infant's chest; the vertebral fractures could be caused by violent shaking of the infant, whose unstable neck would allow his head to thrash back and forth; and the skull fractures with a brain hemorrhage, as determined by autopsy, and the broken arm and leg could be the result of being thrown to the floor. All pointed to a deliberate cause of death. As physicians, we are legally mandated, under penalty, to report child abuse. In this case, we suspected homicide.

The police and district attorney's office eventually were able to illicit a confession from the baby's sobbing, broken-down mother. She had been miserable after her husband walked out on her and her three-week-old infant, leaving her without any funds. Her husband's brother, who had always liked her, came to the rescue. He moved into her apartment and, soon after, into her bed. She was very grateful for the financial help and for his assuming "fatherly care" of her child. Despite being healthy, the infant cried incessantly and made them both frantic. Nothing they did would pacify him. They would squeeze and shake him in desperation. One night when the mother was at work, the baby's uncle threw him to the floor then called her to tell her what had happened. They were both accused and charged with child abuse and the baby's death.

DIANE

Another time in the ER, an eight-year-old girl was brought in at 5:00 A.M. by a neighbor. The child had two swollen eyes, a bloody nose and a swollen ear. She would not tell us what had happened to her. She didn't have to. It was obvious. Even pain-killers could not quell her sobbing. The neighbor blurted out the fact that she had heard intermittent screams from next door for most of the night. This latest episode was not the first time in her memory. Ever since the girl and her parents had moved into the duplex six months ago, she had sporadically heard loud noises and bloodcurdling screams, especially on Saturday or Sunday nights. The neighbor was like most of us—she just minded her own business. This time the girl, Diane, came knocking on her door for help. She was compelled to respond. Our medical findings went beyond her visibly injured eyes, nose and ear, as the physical examination and x-rays would reveal. Her front teeth had two large chips; there was blood in her ear canal (a perforated ear drum); and the skin of her back and buttocks evidenced several recently healed linear scars. The x-rays showed old fractures of three fingers, one wrist and the lower arm. The sum total of Diane's injuries signified acute and chronic physical abuse. We could cure her physical damages but not her emotional wounds. She was admitted to the hospital, as much for her protective custody as for the medical surgical treatment she required. The police were dispatched to find the parents. The child protective authorities would investigate the circumstances of her home life and present their information and impressions to the district attorney. When Diane revealed to a befriended social worker that her father and her mother had been beating her for the past two years, our dreaded suspicions were verified. The neighbor's testimony, if she could rally the courage to come forth, and our medical evidence substantiated a case of abuse that would be presented to the court for prosecution and intervention. The latter was more important. If the parents could be rehabilitated, thereby curing whatever possessed them to beat Diane, the family that she needed could be left intact. By the time Diane was ready for hospital discharge, none of the above had happened. Where would she go? Because of the impending action against her parents, it seemed unconscionable to return her home. The neighbor, who had provided a recent refuge for her mother, was fearful of repercussions from the father. Until matters were resolved, social service's only solution was a foster home for Diane, where she would have a protective setting but as yet an indeterminate future.

EDDIE AND JOSHUA

Lapses in bowel or bladder control in the three- to five-year-old age group are a frequent cause of physical punishment by the parent or caretaker. Eddie's mother had just had her modest home fully carpeted with a most expensive and luxurious covering, for which she and her husband had carefully budgeted. Having gone through successful toilet training for three-year-old Eddie—and even their puppy—they thought it would be safe to start living the formal life-style to which they were accustomed before the late onset of a family. Within twelve hours, the nonadult and non-human forces in their home combined efforts to ruin the plush carpeting. Previously neat, clean and well-behaved little Eddie defecated on the new carpet, right in the middle of the living room floor. He and the dog playfully rolled the soft feces around, tracking it over a wide area. All of this happened between 4:00 and 5:00 A.M. Saturday morning while the parents, out late the night before, slept soundly, never hearing a peep that would have alerted them. Needless to say, they awoke to a mess as they stumbled from their bedroom; she, on her way toward the kitchen to make breakfast and he, on his way to letting the dog out, were both struck by the smell and sight of the smeared carpet. She screeched. He roared. Both vented their common reaction with rage. As soon as Eddie's father had gone outside with the dog, his mother whipped Eddie with a coat hanger, inflicting deep welts wherever the metal landed on his struggling body.

The dog fared better in the father's hands; he was merely confined to the outdoors or the garage for a week. Priorities, priorities—the value of a carpet versus the value of a son.

In another case, a four-year-old boy named Joshua quietly slipped out of the bathtub while his dad answered a phone call. Mom was out shopping. Dripping suds and naked, he ran around the house, jumping on furniture and having a grand old time before his dad caught up with him, at which point Joshua just stood in the middle of his parents' big bed and urinated. That did it. Innocent play turned to violence. His father took off his belt and viciously beat his son. He, as Eddie's mother had done, covered up his shameful loss of control from his spouse. Just one incident of losing control on the part of a parent in disciplining his or her child can be fatal.

INCIDENCE OF PHYSICAL ABUSE

The US Department of Health and Human Services (DHHS), delegated to implement the Child Abuse Prevention and Treatment Act, defines physical abuse as "characterized by inflicting physical injury by punching, beating, kicking, biting, burning or otherwise harming a child. Although the injury is not an accident, the parent or caretaker may not have intended to hurt the child. The injury may have resulted from over-discipline or physical punishment that is inappropriate to the child's age." In its last national report of the incidence of physical abuse (1986), it identified verifiable cases to a total 358,300 children or 5.7 children per 1,000. DHHS concedes that its data are probably a low estimate of the true incidence of abuse since there is no exact method of ascertaining unreported cases. The recent wave of violent behavior and drug and alcohol usage leading to uninhibited behavior make an increased incidence of abuse these days not only likely but probable, as evidenced by state reports.

Oh well, one might think, an occasional outburst of rage taken out on a child or someone else is excusable, "part of human nature." But is it? Or is man, as the most highly developed creature of the animal kingdom, innately violent? I think not. I suggest that if violence is a learned behavior, it can be unlearned or at least controlled. Hot-headed, overreactive responses have no place in the home, community or in dealings between nations. If our goal as parents is to raise a kind and mentally healthy generation, we must set an example. Every day infants and children are abused in our own neighborhoods and right under our own noses while we, like the famous monkeys (see no evil, hear no evil and speak no evil) shun involvement and "mind our own business." Are the abusers the only ones at fault?

CHAPTER 6

THEY'RE NOT OKAY

EMOTIONAL/PSYCHOLOGICAL
ABUSE AND NEGLECT

Who among us has not said a vicious word out of anger and frustration to our children? Did we mean it? Yes, at that moment in time, we probably did. Years later, we are able to painfully recall the hurtful things that our own parents or teachers said to us, yet most of us have survived to become relatively successful adults without psychological hang-ups. In fact, some of us took unkind labels, such as "bad boy/bad girl" or "stupid," "dumb," or "idiot," as challenges to prove them wrong. We became exemplary persons or overachievers. Most of us also vowed that we would not belittle or intentionally hurt our own children. If we were chronically abused or neglected, however, the chances are that we will follow our parental role models and become abusers.

EMOTIONAL/PSYCHOLOGICAL ABUSE

More than 34 percent of American children are subjected to severe and habitual (day in and day out) emotional abuse, according to a US Department of Health and Human Services (DHHS) statistics report from 1986. Varying degrees of emotional and psychological abuse accompany every form of child abuse and neglect.

DHHS defines emotional abuse to "...include acts or omissions by the parents or other persons responsible for the child's care that have caused, or could cause serious behavioral, cognitive, emotional or mental disorders." Psychological abuse is one of the hardest to prove, not only because each child tends to react differently depending on his or her age and makeup but the symptoms of emotional abuse or neglect may take years to surface. More specifically, the National Center for Child Abuse and Neglect describes three major categories of emotional abuse (US DHHS 1988, 4–8):

CLOSE CONFINEMENT (Tying or binding and other forms): torturous restriction of movement, as by tying a child's arms or legs together or binding a child to a chair, bed or other object, or confining a child to an enclosed area (such as a closet) as a means of punishment;

VERBAL OR EMOTIONAL ASSAULT: habitual patterns of belittling, denigrating, scapegoating or other nonphysical forms of overtly hostile or rejecting treatment, as well as threats of other forms of maltreatment (such as threats of beating, sexual assault, abandonment, etc.);

OTHER OR UNKNOWN ABUSE: overtly punitive, exploitative or abusive treatment other than those specified under other forms of abuse or unspecified abusive treatment. This form includes attempted or potential physical or sexual assault, deliberate withholding of food, shelter, sleep or other necessities as a form of punishment, economic exploitation and unspecified abusive actions.

Emotional abuse is the second most frequent "category" of child abuse recorded by the last National Incidence Study: 211,100 children or 3.4 children per 1,000 (US DHHS 1989, 4).

ALCOHOLISM AS A FACTOR IN CHILD ABUSE

As a group, the largest number of children who are abused or neglected grew up having one or more alcoholic parents. Those children who were not physically or sexually abused suffered from psychological and/or emotional abuse or neglect. Whether rich or poor, educated or uneducated, a top-level professional or an unskilled laborer, white or nonwhite, parents and caretakers who are alcohol and drug abusers negatively influence their children, genetically or environmentally. If you don't believe it, just listen to the thousands of testimonies from persons attending AA, AlAnon and AlaTeen. Tragically, the highest rates of alcoholism and other drug abuse occur in the twenty- to twenty-nine-year-olds (rates for males are 33.6 percent and for females 25.8 percent); next highest are the thirty- to thirty-nine-year-olds with rates of 18.7 percent (males) and 9.8 percent (females). Both age spans encompass the childbearing and child rearing years. Divorce occurs in 40 percent of families with alcohol problems and 5.7 million cases per year of family violence are alcohol-related (Kane 1989, 3 no. 4:1-2).

While there are many causes of alcoholism, a genetic predisposition stands out as particularly significant: alcohol preference can be selectively bred in experimental animals; sons and brothers of severely alcoholic men demonstrate a 25 to 50 percent lifetime risk of alcoholism; if one identical twin develops alcoholism, there is a 55 percent or greater chance that the other twin will be alcoholic (McKusick 1986, 33). The following is a somewhat typical story.

MARIO AND ROSA

Mario was a twenty-five-year-old alcoholic father of two small children: Mario, Jr., age five, and Rosa, age three, both robust and active kids. Mario's father had been an alcoholic who was physically abusive to his wife and children. During his father's fits of drunken rage, Mario had often been on the receiving end of his belt, sometimes without provocation. Mario promised himself when his babies were born that he would never hurt them, but when his children raced, yelling and screaming, around the small apartment incessantly during those evenings and weekends that he was baby-sitting for his wife while she was waitressing, his parental coping skills would fade with the consumption of a few beers. Although he maintained enough control not to bodily harm them, he resorted to tying Rosa to her high chair and to locking Mario, Jr., in a dark closet. He would then leave the apartment until their loud crying calmed down. Never did he realize that his disciplinary methods were just as harmful as physical punishment and as long-lasting. Mario, Jr. was plagued by a morbid fear of the dark and closed doors throughout his adolescence and adulthood, requiring psychotherapy for his phobias. Rosa became tactile defensive to the extent that any kind of hug or hand/arm grasp resulted in a scream. She fended off all adults except her mother. The effects on Rosa extended in time to feeling uncomfortable about any body touching at all, a subconscious characteristic that lasted a lifetime, drastically blocking intimate heterosexual relationships. Although Mario's punishment techniques were effective short-term in controlling his children, the long-term repercussions were devastating.

PAUL

Ever since Paul was born, he, unlike Mrs. Johnson's subsequent two sons, appeared to be a clone of his father in face, hair, body build, gait and mannerisms. The resemblance was so strong that his mother often called him "Chuck," his father's name. Because her husband was away from home a great deal as a traveling salesman, she demanded more of Paul, in terms of chores and adult-type responsibilities, than most firstborn children. In return he received more praise and affection than his siblings. This fact, along with being treated as the "man of the house" at the tender age of six, made him very happy. Other than a few difficulties with his school and neighborhood peers for being too bossy, he did well until his parents' marriage started to break up. Chuck was away from home more and more, even weekends on occasion. Mrs. Johnson suspected him of having an extramarital affair. He emphatically denied it, but due to his wife's distrust, the marital bed soon cooled. Mrs. Johnson's frustration and anger during his absences gradually spilled over upon his readily available likeness, Paul. During this time, her criticism of Paul's every effort to help her manage the house and her brothers deteriorated into scapegoating. Since a child of eight could scarcely be expected to understand that his mother's treatment of him was a displacement of her hostility for her husband, Paul was confused and deeply hurt. He had no one to turn to for support. His father was seldom around and his mother had started to drink heavily, aggravating the entire situation. The outward signs of his pain showed in his behavior at school: his classwork deteriorated, he repeatedly got into trouble with the teachers by talking back and being generally unruly and with the kids by bullying and fighting. At home he desperately tried to get back into his mother's favor by assuming more household chores and supervision of his younger brothers, all to no avail. The school principal and guidance counselor contacted Mrs. Johnson about Paul's problems at school. This only made her angrier toward her husband, whom she blamed for just about everything that was going wrong. The result was that she continued to vent her wrath upon Paul. Paul's life at home was literally hell with her constant belittling, berating and scapegoating. He still could not understand how his adoring mother could have changed into such a "wicked witch." Further incidents at school prompted the guidance counselor to request that he be psychologically evaluated. Mrs. Johnson refused. (She had tried to keep her marital difficulties and her alcoholism a secret and was afraid that an evaluation would reveal her own problems.)

Chuck was home so infrequently that he was unaware of Paul's troubles. On one of his rare visits, he came across the school notices regarding Paul's behavior. When he attempted to question his wife about the matter, she became enraged and accused him of being the cause of what had happened to Paul and to herself. He reacted by walking out after making it clear to her and an eavesdropping Paul that he wouldn't be back. It was then that Paul's school misbehavior turned to school phobia: he couldn't take the chance of losing his mother, too, even if she was mean to him. In turn, his mother changed dramatically. Somehow with her greatest ultimate fear—divorce—out in the open and inevitable, she seemed relieved. She stopped drinking and reverted to her former benign relationship with her son. Her previous hostility toward Paul was now focused directly upon her spouse. She started to reorganize her life and sought assistance from a psychotherapist. Gradually realizing that Paul had suffered as well and that his school phobia had to be addressed by a professional, she consented to have him evaluated. Psychotherapy proceeded ever so slowly in resolving Paul's problems. However, for the most part, he was able to attend school regularly and catch up with his classwork. A year or so after the divorce was final, Mrs. Johnson started to date an old friend who liked children and was emotionally supportive of her single-parent situation. Having an adult partner with whom to share home and parenting responsibilities for the first time, she let go of Paul, freeing him to become the child of ten that he was. She hoped it was not too late. (Would that it were that similar cases ended so favorably.)

BED-WETTING AND OTHER BEHAVIORAL ABERRANCIES

When parents deal with a child's developmental or behavioral aberrancy by ridicule or outright anger, it usually results in psychological damage to the child. Thumb-sucking, masturbation in public, soiling underpants and bed-wetting beyond certain ages are some of the common behaviors that evoke exaggerated responses in certain parents. They create humiliation and shame so hurtful to the child that transitory habits become chronic problems. For instance, enuresis, or involuntary urination after the age at which bladder control should have been acquired, is a common but complex problem. After the age of five, it becomes a downright embarrassment and nuisance for the parent; for the child, it may be a nemesis! Bed-wetting, or nocturnal enuresis, is prevalent enough to warrant discussion; 8 percent of school-age children suffer from this condition (Nelson 1983, 73–74). Bladder control at night normally follows soon after daytime control, with some time range. Bed-wetting occurs in two forms, depending upon the time of onset: the *persistent* form, in which a child has never obtained night control and a *regressive* form, in which a child who has been dry for long periods suddenly starts to wet at night. The latter is almost always related to some stressful event in the child's life: a new baby sibling, parental discord, loss of a loved one, a traumatic experience, such as a car accident or hospitalization, moving to a strange environment, or trouble at school. Regressive bed-wetting, depending on how it's managed, is usually transitory. That's not to say that it should not be investigated by a pediatrician, if only to rule out urinary tract infection, particularly in girls who are more prone to infections because of their anatomy and bowel movement wiping techniques of back to front. (Bladder infections usually present symptoms around the clock and are not confined to nocturnal incontinence.) Persistent bed-wetting is a much more serious problem deserving professional attention, medical and psychological. The cause for persistent bed-wetting, according to accepted theory, is insufficient, harsh or unsuitable toilet training combined with prolonged psychological stress in the child's environment. Organic pathology is rare. The existence of multiple treatments for persistent bed-wetting testifies to the complexity of the problem; no one cure is effective for every child or adolescent.

ELOISE

Eloise was a persistent bed-wetter when I saw her at age seventeen on another matter. She had been through the gamut of medical and psychological evaluations and therapies without success. Her family background had been tumultuous: her mother had become seriously ill after the birth of Eloise, her third child. From the time that Eloise was twenty months through four years old, her care was exclusively relinquished to her grandmother, who came to live with the family. That period was critical to her toilet training. Although she can't recall any events during that time, it may be assumed from other information that the trouble started then. Grandma was described as a kind but rigid person of the "old school" who ran the household and upbringing of her three grandchildren like a drill sergeant. Consistent with all her other jobs, she assumed Eloise's toilet training with persistence and zeal. Apparently, her somewhat harsh techniques, judged by modern standards, were two-thirds successful (daytime bladder and bowel control but not nighttime control). It was likely that Grandma did not appreciate the extra laundry burden of her grand- daughter's bed-wetting. Consequently, Eloise was kept in diapers at night throughout her preschool years. When her mother became well enough to take up a full parenting role, Eloise, still bed- wetting, was age seven. She was evaluated by the family doctor who prescribed medication (Tofranil) without a measurable effect. Next, the doctor referred Eloise to a urologist for extensive exam- inations, x-rays and tests (which is one of the worst things he might have done under the circumstances). She remembered the exam procedures as painful and embarrassing. Since her family made an issue of her problem, she had no choice but to cooperate. As one would have suspected, the exams and tests were negative for pathology. Now what? One remedy after another was tried, including liquid restriction after 4:00 P.M., waking her up at 3:00 A.M., an electronic signaling sheet for wetness and a parade of psychologists (one of whom actually created more hostility between parent and child). As Eloise grew older and the habit continued, her parents became disgusted. They couldn't resist ridiculing and humiliating her. The stigma of her bed-wetting prohibited her from going to summer camp or pajama parties, which was allowed for her siblings. She was so ashamed of herself that it affected her whole personality and restricted her social life.

NED

Another child I'll call Ned was brought by his mother into a psychological counselling group where I was consulting. Ned, age six, had encopresis (the involuntary passage of feces beyond the age when control should have been acquired). Like bed-wetting, it is seldom organic in origin but rather a symptom of underlying emotional problems requiring psychotherapy. According to his exasperated mother, he had been soiling his underpants for years and at the same time was chronically constipated. He had been very resistive toward her attempts at his toilet training, having temper tantrums and becoming almost hysterical whenever he was made to sit on the potty. Ned's encopresis was jeopardizing his first-grade school experience. Whenever the teacher detected his offensive odor, she would send him out of the room to the toilet, where he would remain until the nurse or his mother came in with clean underpants. It didn't take long before the other kids caught on. They cruelly teased and taunted him. He soon became known as "stinky-poo" and no one would befriend him. He was absolutely miserable. At home he became more overtly hostile toward his mother. The only temporary solution was to withdraw him from school until the soiling could be cured. His pediatrician's evaluation failed to discover a pathological cause of his problem and thus, he was referred for psychological assessments. Because the psychologist was not getting anywhere after several sessions, I was asked to see Ned in the event that I might find a quicker remedy. The previous pediatrician's report had indicated that Ned's withholding of stool had not progressed to psychogenic megacolon (enlarged colon) as yet, which was a good sign. Knowing that the fecal soiling was an involuntary overflow from his self-willed constipation, I set upon clearing up the constipation. With his mother's cooperation, I instituted a regimen of daily enemas and stool softeners for the first week and a decreased regimen for the following weeks. Two weeks later, his mother returned with Ned to tell me that despite this most distasteful treatment, she was delighted with the early results: no more soiled underwear. With this beginning, he could return to school and proceed with his psychotherapy, an absolutely necessary process for a permanent resolution. In the meantime, not only did Ned escape his mother's verbal wrath by not soiling his pants, he assumed conscious control over his bowel movements, gained social acceptance and was feeling better about himself.

THROWAWAYS

Young people who suffer the most extreme psychological abuse, the ultimate rejection, are those thrown out of their homes by parents who sense that they "can't take it anymore." Such children differ from the runaways who are fleeing from domestic abuse and make their own choice in leaving. Thrown-out youngsters, no matter what the reasons, have been told to leave—their parents have made the choice for them. Their fate on the streets parallels the voluntary runaway. These youngsters, depending upon the reasons for rejection (such as drugs, alcohol or rebellious behavior), tend to fare worse because they have been told that they are not loved by the only persons whom they thought they could count on, a mom or a dad. Locked out physically and emotionally, their sense of self-value approximates zero and facilitates self-destructive behavior of the most severe degree.

DICK

At the age of fourteen, Dick was thrown out of his home by his stepfather and his mother. Dick's biological father had died when he was ten years old, leaving Dick and his mother without adequate funds and having to struggle for quite a while. After his mother married Harry, he was excited to have a man at home to fill the void left by his father's death. Dick was especially happy for his lonely mother. Harry, a real macho guy, took him fishing and hunting. Everything seemed to be going so well until Dick overheard remarks in the boy's locker room concerning his step-father's "whoring around." The town was small, and the gossiping jocks who hang out on the streets had seen Dick's stepfather pick up prostitutes on more than one occasion. Before Dick would believe what he had heard, he wanted to confirm the gossip. He secretly followed Harry whenever he left the house at night. After a few unrevealing pursuits, he actually did observe Harry picking up a prostitute outside the local bar. Now that he had verified the peer rumors, he didn't know what to do with the unwanted information—how should he handle it in light of his in-love mother's feelings? Should he confront his stepfather with his observations and the prior gossip? No, he thought, maybe he had misinterpreted what he saw. Life at home continued unchanged. He went fishing with Harry; his mother was treated kindly and both Harry and she acted like lovebirds. Dick decided to "cool it," but he couldn't resist the temptation to follow Harry on those nights when he was presumably going out for a long walk or to have a drink with the "boys." Dick witnessed a couple more episodes of his stepfather walking off with known prostitutes. He needed to resolve the problem one way or another! The last time, Dick went right up to Harry and said, "Hello." From Harry, there was silence. The youngster returned home, told his mother about his several observations of Harry's behavior, went straight to his room, locked the door and cried all night. Dick was still awake around midnight and could hear his mom and stepfather's loud arguing voices resounding throughout the house. Emotionally exhausted over his four-month dilemma and the showdown, he escaped into sleep. The next morning, he left the house before his parents were up, not wanting to create more conflict. When he returned from school, he was treated with hostility. He sensed that his mother had accepted Harry's story over his own. From then on, Dick became an unwelcome boarder in his own home. His disillusionment with his stepfather and his mother made him rebellious in a lot of small ways that didn't go unnoticed. Eventually, Harry was able to convince Dick's mother that her son was jeopardizing their relationship. If Dick didn't leave, then he would. His mother made her choice: she gave her son a "generous" $200, told him to find another place to live, and that although she loved him, he should not visit her when Harry was home.

ALICIA

Fifteen-year-old Alicia met with a similar fate. She, like Dick, was basically a "good kid" and a victim of a broken home. Alicia's mother had been murdered during a liquor store robbery some two years before. Father and daughter had each coped with the loss of a loved one in their own ways: he had submerged himself in work; she in community activities with supportive neighbors and school friends. When her father rather suddenly introduced his wife-to-be, it took both Alicia and the neighbors by surprise. The future stepmother was a mere ten years older than

Alicia and a good fifteen years younger than her father. She was more like a big sister than a mother replacement. The stepdaughter became the bride's maid-of-honor at the civil marriage ceremony in the justice of the peace's parlor. Alicia felt very grown up. She mimicked her young stepmother, Mary Ann, in mannerisms, makeup and dress. It appeared that everything was going well and they had a lot of "girl talks" regarding the "dos" and "don'ts" of behavior with boys and men. Alicia was ecstatic with Mary Ann's company. It was great to have her father home more regularly. Always having been popular at school, Alicia's new image now attracted the older boys. Several months after the marriage, however, Mary Ann seemed to be turning against her stepdaughter. Was it too much when Alicia flaunted her eighteen-year-old boyfriends before her? Mary Ann also noticed that some of her makeup, birth control pills and clothes were missing from time to time. She confronted Alicia about these various matters. Mary Ann met absolute denial of her accusations and a certain hostility between them was seeded. When Alicia became defensively sassy and obstinate, a shouting scene ensued. Her young stepmother, once her friend, became her adversary and convinced her husband that Alicia was no longer his innocent daughter. The final straw in alienating Mary Ann and her father was when she brought a twenty-five-year-old man (same age as her father's wife) home to meet them. Alicia's date was asked to leave and ordered not to see this fifteen-year-old again. Alicia threw a tantrum, repeatedly using profane language; her father called her a tramp and a disgrace to her dead mother and Mary Ann interjected with her previous complaints. It was clearly two against one. The next morning, heads cool but not forgiving, Alicia was handed a one-way airplane ticket to go to live with a distant aunt whom she'd never met. She took the ticket and left, not for the airport but for the streets.

PARENTAL ALIENATION SYNDROME

"The parental alienation syndrome" was described by Dr. Richard A. Gardner in his book, *Child Custody Litigation: A Guide for Parents and Mental Health Professionals* (Gardner 1986, 76-104). Dr. Gardner highlights several forms of emotional/ psychological child abuse surfacing with significant prevalence during the last decade. The rise in such abuse he attributes to the increase in court battles over joint child custody, which had not been an issue previously; in the past, the court had awarded sole custody to the mother without much objection from father. More often than fathers, mothers brainwash their younger children with various conscious or unconscious techniques against their estranged parent, using hostile misrepresentation or fabrication, and actually creating "hatred" of him in the child's mind. The child's public acting-out behavior against the opposite parent (who may in fact have been the better parent, more sensitive, devoted, nurturing and supportive) are so overtly explosive with vehement and false accusations that such demonstrations tend to fool and deceive mental health professionals, attorneys and judges. To cause unwarranted alienation in a child toward a loving parent and his or her extended family (grandparents, aunts, uncles, nieces and nephews) does a cruel disservice to the youngster. It deprives the child of a potentially loyal support system and good role models that can rarely be replicated. The parental alienation syndrome in this context overshoots its target: the maligned parent. It deprives grandparents of any relationship with grandchildren, sometimes permanently. Children of divorcing parents usually have already experienced major trauma by the common predivorce parental arguments, hostility and physical absence of their father. Now their own anger is compounded with their mother's by her manipulations. Any number of overt or subtle maneuvers, ranging from outright lies through delusional accusations and threats of poverty, are used to turn the child against his or her father. Often heard are fallacious accusations of drunkenness, drug usage, beatings, extra-marital affairs and abandonment. Perhaps the most vicious technique involves the fabrication of charges of child sexual molestation in which the child becomes the innocent accomplice. The consequences to the child as well as the parent are profound and long-lasting.

Subtle techniques of creating an alienation complex in the child are one parent's interception of telephone calls, mail or presents from the other to the child. These techniques clearly aim at proving to the child that the absent parent no longer cares for him or her. The unfortunate secondary effects are that they substantiate the child's guilt feelings that he or she was the cause of the divorce. Frequently, the nondeliberate instigator of alienation subconsciously impacts the child against an ex-mate with hostile negatives that slip out in voice tones and "innocent" rhetoric. Many psychiatrists think that subtle or unconscious alienation techniques are more effective to the child's orientation than overt or deliberate ones. Whether or not the alienating techniques are major or minor, deliberately plotted or unconsciously blurted out, "messing with a child's mind" in this way is destructive and psychologically scarring. The awareness of outside observers and professionals of this ubiquitous, ever-escalating parental alienation phenomenon (more than 90 percent in Dr. Gardner's experience with custody suits) may result in early intervention before further harm is done to the child—and his parents.

A good friend of mine, a lawyer who specializes in domestic relations, can cite many examples of the parental alienation syndrome in her practice. Because of her past experience in early childhood development training and teaching, she, unlike most attorneys, was more perceptive to divorce-related trauma in the child.

BOBBY————————————————————————————————

One of her clients had a nine-year-old boy who was the victim of a joint-custody suit. Bobby was the only child of a couple who had fought for years. His mother had given up her career as a retail fashion buyer for a large chain store to take care of Bobby, a fact that generated huge resentment when the marriage failed. The boy listened daily to his mother's berating of his father. Bobby shocked the lawyers and the court with his use of profanity toward his father; at home, he covetously hid a few of his father's possessions that hadn't been destroyed by his mother in her spitefulness. My friend understood this dichotomy in his feelings. Bobby's mother insisted upon sole custody. The court battle would be long and painful unless the parties could quiet their emotions and be rational. The attorney was able to persuade the mother to get psychiatric help for herself and Bobby. With the cooperation of the father's lawyer, she was able to delay the divorce proceedings until the child custody issue could be more equitably mediated. Too many other cases of acrimonious divorce and battles for child custody have a less desirable result for the child. Often divorce court judges and attorneys are insensitive to the child's best interests and the destructive games parents play.

EMOTIONAL/PSYCHOLOGICAL NEGLECT

The most recent DHHS study (1986) found that emotional neglect was the least frequently documented type of child neglect (223,000 children or 3.5 per 1,000). It followed first by physical neglect (571,000 or 9.1 per 1,000 children) and then by educational neglect (292,100 or 4.6 per 1,000 children). The DHHS bureaucracy recognizes some seven specific forms of emotional neglect, defined as follows:

INADEQUATE NURTURING/AFFECTION: marked inattention to the child's needs for affection, emotional support, attention or competence;

CHRONIC/EXTREME SPOUSE ABUSE: chronic or extreme spouse abuse or other domestic violence in the child's presence;

PERMITTED DRUG/ALCOHOL ABUSE: encouragement or permitting of drug or alcohol use by the child (cases of the child's drug/alcohol use were included here if it appeared that the parent/guardian had been informed of the problem and had not attempted to intervene);

PERMITTED OTHER MALADAPTIVE BEHAVIOR: encouragement or permitting of other maladaptive behavior (such as severe assaultiveness, chronic delinquency) under circumstances where the parent/guardian had reason to be aware of the existence and seriousness of the problem but did not attempt to intervene;

REFUSAL OF PSYCHOLOGICAL CARE: refusal to allow needed and available treatment for a child's emotional or behavioral impairment or problem in accord with competent professional recommendation;

DELAY IN PSYCHOLOGICAL CARE: failure to seek or provide needed treatment for a child's emotional or behavioral impairment or problem which any reasonable laymen would have recognized as needing professional psychological attention (such as severe depression, suicide attempt); and

OTHER EMOTIONAL NEGLECT: other inattention to the child's developmental/emotional needs not classifiable under any of the above forms of emotional neglect (e.g., markedly overprotective restrictions which foster immaturity or emotional overdependence, chronically applying expectations clearly inappropriate in relation to the child's age or level of development).

These definitions alone could put half of the well-meaning parents of the 1970s and 1980s at fault. In light of the current level of funding and the inability of qualified professionals to even deal with the most severe cases of life-threatening physical abuse, it seems unlikely that the more subtle cases of abuse and neglect will get attention. Ironically, most emotionally neglected children go unnoticed and unattended until as adults they surface in mental health facilities.

PARENTAL DEPRIVATION

Nurturant neglect can begin in infancy with "maternal deprivation" leading to failure to thrive or it can express its psychologically devastating effect at any period of childhood.

ROBERTA

Roberta was the victim of parental inattention to her emotional needs throughout most of her formative years. Her parents were involved in the diplomatic corps: her father, the secretary to ambassadors, and her mother, the perennial hostess. Raised primarily by nannies and living overseas without other family, contact with her parents was infrequent and always formal. She recalls attending a string of boarding schools in Europe and that even vacations at home were programmed with official entertaining. She grew up feeling very lonely, unloved and estranged from her parents. She compared herself to an affluent orphan—never having a real home or getting to know her parents. Her young womanhood bespoke of one failed relationship after another: she had two abortions and one suicide attempt. Never having learned how to receive love or to give love was the tragedy of her life.

On a lesser scale of affluence and romantic life style are many middle-class children living with parents who are so insensitive to their emotional needs that the children feel unloved. When they are sent away to residential prep schools, presumably for a better education, the youngsters interpret the process as further rejection.

ANNIE—

Annie's young life demonstrates the whole gamut of emotional abuses and neglects as described by DHHS. She was a continual witness to her mother being beaten up by her father. Father was a hardworking, hard-drinking lumberjack who was away from home weekdays, living at a lumber camp in northern New Hampshire. Annie considered him a good provider for her mom, three sisters and brother. Upon his return home on Fridays, he took them shopping for groceries, clothes and occasionally special presents. He never laid a violent hand on her or the other kids; their worst punishment was being locked out of their parents' bedroom and hearing their mother scream and cry after Annie and her siblings had witnessed her beatings. (In later years, she suspected that her mother was being raped.) After her father was killed in a logging accident, his best friend started to visit them on weekends. Annie was now thirteen. At first his visits were welcomed since he assumed all her dad's good behavior. That was short-lived. Although he did not drink or beat her mother, he smoked pot, sniffed cocaine and dragged her mother off to the bedroom, locking the door. Late at night, she would hear her mother utter the same screams as previously.

Annie and her siblings satisfied their preadolescent curiosity by occasionally stealing a "joint" or two and experimenting. Annie and her brother Bill became habituated. The consequences of this showed up in their sliding school performances, hanging-out with other (abusers) losers and being truant from school. Their mother, now working full-time, failed to respond to the school authorities' requests to discuss Annie's and Bill's problems. (The most dedicated of schoolteachers, guidance counselors and principals will give up on a child when parents fail to show concern.) Annie and Bill ran wild for months, except for weekends when Mom and her boyfriend were at home and taking charge—albeit smoking pot and having sex. To all outside appearances, Annie's mother and friend were providing well for the children.

One night about 11:00 P.M., the local police called Annie's mother from the station to inform her that her daughter and son had been picked up for possession of marijuana and dealing crack-cocaine. She knew her kids had missed their curfew on that particular Wednesday night but she could not believe that they were in trouble with the law. She thought that she and the kids had made such a good recovery from her husband's death and that all of them had been doing fine. Even when confronting the judge in juvenile court, she denied knowledge of their marijuana and crack usage, going so far as to say that they were never exposed to such in her presence. She also turned down the court's offer of a substance abuse rehabilitation program for Annie and Bill.

In disallowing her children the intervention they needed, she essentially condoned their behavior; Annie knew that her mother had lied in court. Parental admonishments to their children to "do as I say, not as I do" or words to that effect have seldom worked. After a few weeks of impressing their mother with good behavior, Annie and Bill reverted to their previous usage. When the school authorities again heard the town gossip substantiating their previous suspicions of Annie's and Bill's drug usage, they contacted their mother. This time she met with them but adamantly refused their recommendation to help her youngsters through counseling. A few weeks later, Annie and Bill ran away and haven't been heard from since.

CURT

Curt was eleven years old when his mother married for a third time. He was the oldest of her three children, the only male issue of her first marriage. Curt had adjusted well to his first stepfather, whom he adored. They would play ball, go fishing or just enjoy quiet times together. He was the only father that Curt had ever really known. His biological parent had deserted the family when the boy was five years old. This treasured father-son relationship came to an abrupt halt when his stepfather was killed in a plane crash. Mother remarried soon after his death, this time to an older man with whom Curt did not feel anywhere near the same companionship. When his sisters got more and more attention from his new stepfather while Curt was asked to do an inordinate amount of the household chores—only to be criticized rather than thanked—he developed a growing resentment and sense of rejection. He also missed the loving and sharing relationship he had had with his previous stepfather.

It wasn't long before his mom presented the family with a new baby. Curt was pushed further aside in preference for this man's own son. No positive attention-getting maneuvers seemed to produce the result that Curt desperately needed: some sign of parental love, so he turned to a negative approach. As an emerging adolescent, he had other resources—mobility outside the home and his friends at school who were experimenting with drugs, stealing and truancy. He proceeded to get into trouble with several department store security guards for shoplifting, with the school authorities for unexcused absences and with the police for being caught in the company of kids possessing drugs. Albeit negative, he succeeded in getting the attention from his mom and stepfather he craved. Confined to the house except for attending school, given more chores without any show of gratitude, and painfully forced to witness the exclusive attention being paid to his sisters and his baby brother by his mother and stepfather, the situation became intolerable to him. Nothing he did seemed to go right.

One Saturday when the others were off for a day's shopping and he was left home to mow the grass and rake the leaves, Curt ran off to join his friends at the ballpark. One thing led to another and he decided to continue having fun into the evening. Who would care if he never came home? Within a day, he and his thirteen-year-old buddy were caught vandalizing a closed record shop. The call from the police to his home was answered by his stepfather, who refused to take him back. He was labeled a delinquent and a stubborn child. His behavior, provoked by his stepfather and his own love-mesmerized mother, had made him a perfect candidate for "dumping"—and that he was, right into the lap of state care. During the social workers' and psychologists' interviews, he was never able to defend his actions or explain his attitude; his home and his parents were assessed as above average in acceptable standards for child rearing. The court, based upon his parents' affidavit of Curt's behavior and the professionals' inconclusive findings of why he did what he did, judged him to be an incorrigible adolescent. He was placed in an institution where he would be provided with a therapeutically constructive confinement, board, room and an "education" of sorts. The latter was more than the academic type of education that may have been intended. He was housed with mostly tough kids, victims of abandonment, who were serious delinquents in the truest sense of the word. His placement was supposed to be reevaluated in a year. Due to bureaucratic slipups and the lack of parental advocacy, it never was. Other than two letters from his mom, saying how sorry she was about him, chatting on and on about her and her husband's and his siblings' happy activities, Curt received no other communication from the outside. His fourteenth birthday and Christmas came and went with only a card for each—no phone calls, no visits, no presents—nothing! That's exactly how he felt, like a nothing!

When his situation came up for review a year later, his record for the two miserable years he had spent at the institution was clean and "promising." The board was convinced that he had been rehabilitated and that he should be free to return home. His stepfather and his mother, having had their second baby, thought otherwise. They felt that the extra stress placed upon their household by Curt would be too much for them, so they denied his home placement. At age fifteen, more than two years after his initial incarceration and four years after his mother's third marriage, he was again being rejected by the only family he had. The state authorities sent him to the first of three foster homes he was to have before he reached the age of eighteen and emancipation, when he promptly enlisted in the armed forces.

PARENTAL OVERPROTECTIVENESS

Emotional neglect in the form of overprotective restrictions that foster immaturity and emotional overdependence is not confined to the "little princesses" or "Lord Fauntleroys" of the affluent segment of our society. They may include the "treasured" single child from any segment, as in the case of Jake.

JAKE——————————————————————————————

Mr. and Mrs. Reid, happily married for eight years, had been trying to conceive a child during almost every month of that time. When Jake, a five-pound baby boy, arrived after Mrs. Reid's three miscarriages, his parents had all their prayers answered. From day one, no extravagance or sacrifice was too great for this taxi driver and his wife—and there were many. Because of Mrs. Reid's fear of Jake catching some childhood illness from exposure to other children, she avoided the neighborhood mother-and-child get-togethers. Consistent with the liberal childbearing philosophy of the 1950s and 1960s in which a child was permitted to act out without restrictions (doing whatever he wanted to, sleeping and eating whenever he felt like it), Mrs. Reid ended up raising a spoiled, unruly little boy rather than the well-adjusted child the formula promised.

Mrs. Reid's smothering and overprotection extended to such things as never letting Jake cry and not giving him room to explore or to learn by trial and error. She never left his side day and night as sole playmate and companion. Mr. Reid bought him the most expensive toys on the market and Jake, in turn, smashed a number of them after his father had spent hours teaching him how to use them. When "precious" Jake started kindergarten, the experience proved to be a disaster. Within a few days, the teacher recommended his withdrawal because of his emotional immaturity and the fact that he was uncontrollable. Another year went by of Jake carrying on with his mother at home, isolated from his peers. When he reentered the school system at age six and a half, Jake continued to be disruptive and immature for his age. An evaluation revealed that he was bright enough to be in a regular classroom but would require one-to-one teaching and intensive work with a child psychologist. His parents gladly paid for private tutoring and therapy—"anything for their son." Gradually, he was able to tolerate small groups of children and by the third grade was able to enter the regular classroom. Getting through to his parents as to how they should treat Jake at home, however, was more difficult; they exhibited frequent relapses and were unable to break themselves of their overindulgent behavior.

Jake's early adolescent years required additional psychotherapy because of several difficulties with his classmate relationships. He was involved in almost daily fights provoked by his arrogance, selfishness and vengeful ways. Having acquired a reputation as a "snitch" and an all-around troublemaker necessitated that his parents transfer him to another junior high school and later to a private school for the emotionally disturbed.

CULTS

If the experts as they are presented in the national media are correct, satanic and other types of cults are on the rise, translating into a real danger to the well-being of our young people. There is evidence confirming that cults have been on the rise in America for the past twenty years (Appel 1983). Perhaps lending credence in some unscientific way to the interest in cults is a statement announced by a so-called expert in satanic history that the satanic bible has exceeded the Christian Bible in sales. My personal experience, in attempting to research the subject in three medium-sized libraries, was to be put on a long waiting list since every book on the matter had been checked out.

The American Heritage Dictionary defines "cult" as: "1. a system or community of religious worship and ritual; 2(a). a religion or religious sect generally considered extremist or bogus." The average person is seldom aware of the prevalence of cults, usually cloaked in secrecy. They confront the reality of cults only when they are shocked by exposés such as the murder-suicide of 911 American adults and children under the mad leadership of the Reverend Jim Jones in Guyana in 1978 or the 1989 finding of masses of adult and children's bones buried over the Texas border in Mexico during a search for a missing American college student. The allegiance of any sane person to cults and their brutal rituals is incomprehensible to most of us.

Endemic to cults is child abuse of the most severe and diversified forms, encompassing murder, castration, drugging, starvation, sleep deprivation, sexual excess or total abstinence and living human or animal sacrifice. Long before the death of all those children and adults in Jonestown, survivors of the sect recalled how the resistant children were treated: they were tied up in the jungle overnight, suspended in deep wells with the threat of drowning, beaten, tortured with electric wire shock or drugged. While the surviving great religions today continue sacramental offerings as pledges of worship, vegetable or fruit derivatives have been substituted for animal and human sacrifices—not so for some cults, however, even in the twentieth century.

Belief in the supernatural, mystical events and miracles is a normal maturational phase of childhood. Codes and rituals peculiar to secret societies allowing members to feel elite; believing in the "good fairy" to leave a coin as a reward for a tooth under the pillow; the mystique of Santa Claus, bringing all the things asked for; wishing upon a star or a chicken breast bone—these are all part of childhood. The world of youthful fantasy delights persons of all ages. It is undoubtedly elemental to creativity in artistic endeavors, the inventiveness of scientists, stories of fiction writers and to imagination in all spheres of human interest. Many children even as they mature cannot distinguish fantasy from reality, a condition that makes them vulnerable to the irrational threats and fears imposed upon them by cult leaders. The gravitation of emotionally immature and insecure young people to cults is well-recognized. The data indicates that such youngsters are in their mid-teens to early twenties, mostly from white, middle-class, intact families, with a male to female ratio of 2:1 (Appel 1983; Ebon 1976). Cult popularity reflects adolescent rebellion mixed with a level of tumultuous fanaticism. What more vulnerable time than adolescence for the confused young person to be seduced by cult dogma? It is a time characterized by the demand to develop individuality, to achieve autonomous separation from family, to question parental and societal values and to form commitments to self as a soon-to-emerge adult.

Who are the youngsters with the highest risk of joining cults? They are average kids who suffer frustration and disappointment when they fail to fulfill their own or their parents' expectations. They are kids who have demonstrated chronic emotional and developmental problems in the past. They are kids who are disillusioned with present-day society and who fail to obtain gratification from their daily lives; some are kids with emotional disturbances so deep that the sadistic rituals of certain cults attract them. For the more serious-minded young person, a fear of nuclear world destruction, the desire to combat materialism personally combined with a dissatisfaction or disagreement with the tenets of conventional religions might motivate him or her to seek salvation in alternative sects.

A youngster's voyage through adolescence, including the natural process of breaking away from parents and authority figures, can be a stormy one for parents as well as children, sometimes ending up in a shipwreck or loss at sea. While cults appear to offer an escape from some troubling concerns about the fate of the universe (such as nuclear disaster, environmental pollution, violence, famine, chemically poisoned food or outright war), authoritarianism, greed and societal rules of conduct, they deceptively function in much the same manner as the conventional society from which the youngster is fleeing. In fact, the rules of conduct, absolute conformity to a particular life style and authoritarian control can be far stricter. Noncompliance or disobedience may be mercilessly punished without the benefit of trial by rational jury. The initial appeal of some cults to the young person for living an uninhibited life and doing as one pleases soon turns into a form of mental, spiritual and physical slavery. Satanic cults attract emotionally unstable personalities who have a tendency toward the physical with their violence and provide group acceptance of human sacrifice.

The messianic cults offer refuge from the "cruel" everyday world of reality with prophecy that a savior will rescue believers. Unlike the conventional time-tested Judaism and Christianity of recent centuries that have shaped societies constructively and given faith and charity to the downtrodden and sick, some modern religions such as the Unification Church, Hare Krishna and the Church of Scientology, to name a few, prey upon the youth's disillusionment with organized society by further alienation. Because some cults have greedy leadership, they have become big business. The followers are a source of free labor and fund solicitation. All cults attract followers who are spiritually starved, basically feeling unloved and thirsting for communal belonging to a paternalistic/maternalistic family, be it supernatural or embodied with human disciples. The seduction of young people through the brainwashing techniques of cults is a psychological abuse of the severest order.

Today many bright yet gullible young men and women are seeking a meaning to life, having been "turned off" by materialism, greed and the fierce competition for top scholastic grades, careers, money and a Yuppie life style. The story that follows can serve as a prototype for the way many young people are mesmerized and entrapped by cults.

BILL

Bill, a nineteen-year-old man from a professionally successful and affluent family, dropped out of college at the midterm of his sophomore year for no other reason than that he was disillusioned by his classmates' life style—partying, cheating on exams and a general lack of purpose. Instead of returning to school after Christmas break at home with his family, he took off to wander around the country. While searching and seeking from city to city, he grew more and more lonely and depressed by what he saw. In the hustle and bustle of the streets and marketplaces, he witnessed rudeness and unkindness as well as the pushing and shoving to get through doors first on transit systems or to queue up for restaurant seating; the officiousness and petty competition in business offices; and the flagrant demonstrations of sexual seduction in the drinking bars. About three months into his voyage, Bill was befriended by Henry, another disillusioned college dropout, who invited him to a weekend retreat. There Bill met other young men and women who were straight and serious-minded. Their Saturday night party was pot, alcohol and drug free, overtly sexless and generally wholesome. It was those meaningful discussions in the bull sessions that interested him the most. The entire atmosphere was in marked contrast to what Bill had experienced in college. He liked it! Upon his return to the city, he made up his mind to stay around and extended his one-room apartment lease for a month. Henry and one or two of his other new friends would drop in frequently at night, after work or on weekends for more discussions. Later on, he was invited to large group meetings where people searching for a meaning to life and dedication to a cause were assembled. Before he knew what was happening to him, he was "in"—not comprehending what was happening until it was too late. Bill found himself quitting his job, giving up his apartment and moving to a rural communal compound with his friends. There, he worked all day and was bombarded all night with those "meaningful discussions," which were essentially cult indoctrinations, allowing little time to sleep or think or evaluate what was going on.

Since Bill's parents had not heard from him in months and his last letter sounded strange, they started a search. Their private detective, relying upon the postmark of his last letter, eventually tracked Bill down. His parents flew 1,500 miles into the airport nearest to Bill's reported location; they rented a van and, after two days of staking out the compound, literally stormed the fenced-in farm, led by the private detective and his hired strong-arms. Once they found Bill they couldn't believe what they saw. Was this confused, gaunt, childlike person the independent son they had known? Deprogramming took effect more rapidly than they had anticipated compared to other cases, but Bill was a psychological wreck for a long time.

PARENTAL KIDNAPPING

The case where a child is kidnapped from the custody of a parent by an estranged parent falls within the realm of emotional/psychological abuse. The motivation for the kidnapping is important in terms of the child's welfare: parental love of the child versus kidnapping out of spousal revenge or in defiance of the court order. These children are usually young, mostly preschool ages. If the kidnapper's motive is love of their child and rescue from the custody parent whom he or she considers neglectful or abusive, the child's emotional trauma from the abrupt separation may be minimal; on the other hand, if the kidnapper's motive is vengeful and sadomasochistic, irreparable emotional trauma is inevitable as the child is used as a pawn and exploited for any number of devious purposes.

SHARON

Sharon was taken from a local shopping mall by her divorced daddy who loved her and couldn't tolerate restrictive, limited visitations. Since his acrimonious separation and divorce from Sharon's mother, he had learned that his ex-wife, mother of his only child, was neglecting Sharon by leaving her in the care of baby-sitters for two to four days and nights while she played the field of male acquaintances. After the judge's ruling, giving the primary custody of Sharon to her mother, he had dearly missed seeing her. His visitation was confined to a few hours every two weeks and even this brief time was missed occasionally when he could not reach her mother. Sharon's father, a bank teller, couldn't afford the legal fees for another custody battle. His solution was to resign his job at the bank, pay his bills and snatch his precious child. He traveled out of state for many hundreds of miles to a temperate, sunny location where he readily got work as a part-time carpenter and handyman. He made sure that Sharon was loved. Seldom was she left to the care of others. Although he had never tried to hide or conceal his identity, it didn't matter. Sharon's mother never reported her daughter missing to the authorities or tried to find her.

ROBIN

In marked contrast to Sharon's experience was that of Robin, who, at five years of age and with all her mother's beauty, was the victim of a prolonged divorce and custody dispute. Ultimately, she was kidnapped by her foreign father. Robin had been born to affluent parents. Her mother, a graduate of an elite women's school in the eastern United States, met her future husband, Mr. Gabr, an Egyptian, during a vacation on Saint Marten when she was twenty-three. Within a year, they were married and Robin was conceived—despite the fact that her white, Anglo parents heartily disapproved of him. Robin's mother and her husband were very happy during the first two years of their marriage. She carried on with her postdebutante social life while being a wife and mothering her tiny daughter; her husband pursued his postgraduate studies in scientific technology at MIT. During their third marital year, they lost his highly desired male baby due to fetal death. Robin's mother reacted with a deep depression. This tragedy, aggravated by the fact that her parents were constantly interfering with the couple's lives and Robin's rearing, laid the groundwork for marital discord. Mr. and Mrs. Gabr seemed to be fighting all the time. Robin's mother gravitated more and more toward her parents' adversarial position to her husband. Divorce proceedings had been initiated by the time Mr. Gabr had finished his American studies and planned to return to Egypt. Mother and child moved out of their apartment and into her folks' home. Mr. Gabr left the country in anger, taking all the money they had in their joint bank account. Little more than two months after the final divorce decree, awarding sole custody of Robin to her mother, the toddler was kidnapped. Without any prior warning about his intended action (in fact, they had heard no word from him in a year), Mr. Gabr returned to the States. He watched Robin's grandparents' estate for four days. Then, in the few minutes when Robin was playing alone on the periphery of the grounds, he snatched her.

Her mother, grandparents and the police initially thought that Robin had wondered off on the twenty-acre wooded property or perhaps had fallen into one of the duck ponds. Their frantic search turned up no sign of her, no scraps of clothing or toys. Nothing. The grounds search being futile, they had to suspect foul play. Who and why were the haunting questions. It was a full day after her disappearance that the postman delivered the revealing letter from Mr. Gabr, postmarked the day before and in their own town. The letter stated that he had taken Robin, his "rightful property," and left the United States; he said that they would never see her again, that his influential friends in Egypt would see to it that Robin never returned and that her mother and grandparents should not try to retrieve her. His threats did not stop Robin's mother or her grandparents from hiring international detectives to find her. They exerted their influence on US congressmen to act on Robin's behalf. During the next four years, their efforts were unsuccessful. (Robin would have been nine years old by then.) Robin's mother, once again suffering the loss of a child, sank into a depression. Robin's fate remains unknown.

AARON AND ADAM

Mr. and Mrs. Gregory were the parents of twin boys, the products of a late first marriage for both. Mrs. Gregory was thirty-nine and Mr. Gregory forty-nine when the boys were born. He had a successful private law practice, cultivated many friendships with politicians in "high places" and at forty had been appointed a judge. Mrs. Gregory had gone from a master's level social worker in public service to a graduate registered nurse and nursing school faculty prior to their union. Having a child, let alone two normal babies in her advanced maternal age, surpassed her greatest hope. When the twins arrived, she dropped everything at work to stay at home, love and nurture them. Aaron and Adam were quite the full-time job, "double trouble and double joy," leaving her near exhaustion day after day. While the boys' father was helpful for the first year and a half, he gradually drifted away from the children and his wife, arriving home late at night and often spending weekends away for "professional conferences."

Mrs. Gregory never concerned herself about his infrequent lovemaking. In fact, prior to their marriage their relationship had been exclusively platonic. As the twins approached the age of four years, Judge Gregory seemed to renew his earlier interest in them and even in his wife on occasion. Mrs. Gregory resumed her nursing career part-time and worked the 11:00 P.M. to 7:00 A.M. shift three times a week. By the time she went to work and their father was settling in at home, Aaron and Adam were always soundly sleeping after their rambunctious day.

One night Mrs. Gregory returned home from work about 2:00 A.M. because she was ill. More than a little surprised, she found her husband having a drink with company—a younger man whom she had never met. After acknowledging his presence, she went straight to the bathroom and then to bed. She noticed that the bathroom and the bed were in disarray. She was sure that she had left them both neat and tidy. Oh well, maybe the twins had gotten up to play with their daddy after she had left for work. In any case, she was too sick to worry about that now.

Mr. Gregory had become an avid photography buff, purchasing extensive professional equipment when the twins were babies. The cameras and tripod were always cluttering up space in their small living room. A space in the basement was allocated as a fully equipped darkroom in which he processed his own film. Aaron and Adam were constantly being photographed with his new audiovideo toy. During one of those weekends when the judge was away, Mrs. Gregory inadvertently discovered a tape in their video cassette recorder that showed her twins frolicking around the house naked and in the bathtub playing with each others genitals.

Needless to say, she was shocked, repulsed and angry to learn that her husband had photographed such a display. It was then that she recalled the scene of household disarray that she had found on the night she had unexpectedly returned home from work. If her husband was a kiddie pornography enthusiast, what else might he be? His lack of interest in making love to her ever since the twins were born gave rise to the question of whether or not he was also a homosexual. She started to put the many suggestive pieces of their life together; the composite picture seen from this newly found perspective left her convinced of her worst suspicions. All Saturday night and Sunday morning she wrestled with her possible course of action. She knew that confronting him with the evidence and her suspicions would only evoke denial and probable rage on his part. She knew that because of his power and influence, her accusations before law enforcement officers or the judiciary would not be effective. Her main interest was in protecting her sons against any further exploitation before real harm could be done. By noon, she had made up her mind, however impulsively. She had to get the twins away from their father! Mrs. Gregory made a long-distance phone call, hurriedly packed their things in the station wagon and left a note saying they'd be away for a few days but not indicating where. She and her sons drove off. The first night on the road they stayed at a motel; by the end of the next day, they had reached her friend's farm house 900 miles from home. After the twins had become familiar with her friend and the other children, Mrs. Gregory returned home to face her husband and to clarify her position and his. When she refused to reveal the location of their children, he accused her of kidnapping. She was convinced that she was protecting her children. Subsequent months would see the children moved from one home to another in order to escape detection by his detectives. Although to my knowledge Aaron and Adam did not experience sexual molestation, they suffered the emotional trauma of missing parents. At this writing the twins' fate is unknown.

Whether children are willfully traumatized psychologically by their parents' denigrating language or whether young people are caught up as victims of marital acrimonious "games," cult seduction or kidnapping, the end result is mental abuse.

CHAPTER 7

I CAN'T TAKE IT ANYMORE!

RUNAWAYS AND SUICIDES

Any one of the previously described cases of child abuse and neglect could have resulted in suicide or the child running away; thus, the justification for including these two subjects in this book. Why a youngster chooses one and not the other can be theorized endlessly by experts in youth sociology, psychology, psychiatry, law enforcement and the judiciary. According to estimates, more than 6,000 teenagers committed suicide in the United States in 1989; these figures represent a 300 percent increase for white males and a 33 percent increase for females during the last fifteen years (Brookside Hospital 1989, 2:1). Also, about one million adolescents attempted suicide (90 percent were girls) and 50 percent of all teenagers have considered it (Sargent 1989). US vital statistics report suicide as the second leading cause of death in adolescents, superseded only by accidents. If the truth be known, a large proportion of "accidental" deaths are probably deliberate attempts to end one's life.

Just as the causes for child abuse are multiple and complex, so are the causes for running away or committing suicide. Whether it is the runaway's "I can't take it anymore" regarding his or her environment or the suicide's "I can't take it anymore" regarding life itself, there are similar internal and external factors that make individual youngsters more likely to do one or the other (Sargent 1989). The factor both have in common is intolerable emotional pain. Among the intrinsic characteristics often identified in runaway or suicidal youth are poor self-esteem, communication breakdowns with the family, severe impulsiveness, erratic moods, confused thinking or substance abuse—35 percent of teenage suicides occur under the influence of alcohol or drugs (Sargent 1989). Common external factors are: trouble with school performance due to attitudinal or learning disabilities; nonacceptance by peers resulting in social isolation; trouble with the law secondary to conduct disorders, loss of a friend or romantic attachment; loss of a loved relative through divorce or death; victimization by rape or other abuse; and unwanted pregnancy (Hafen and Frandsen 1986; Hendin 1982; Langone 1986).

Given that the typical adolescent perceives events and issues in absolute terms (all or nothing), is it any surprise that the more unstable, who lack emotional support, would take drastic measures in their problem solving?

Demonstrations of violence and self-destructive behavior are ubiquitous. It's what we see on television, in movies, on the news, in our communities and sometimes in our homes. Our violent society is reflected in our kids, with their increased rates of self-destructive behavior and depression. To distinguish violence from aggression, a person must acquire discretionary control over his instinctual reflexes, a maturational task that many adults have yet to accomplish. "Violence is aggression out of control," says Dr.

Lee Combrinck-Graham, director of the Institute for Juvenile Research at the University of Illinois (Combrinck-Graham 1989).

Our most popular pastime as a nation is watching or participating in sports (active or passive) which require physical aggressiveness, largely controlled by rules and regulations of conduct. Yet more and more individual players and fans break through contest controls with acts of violence toward one another. Be it in sports, on the streets, in our homes or with organized pro or con issue-oriented groups, violence pervades our society in what statistics tell us are epidemic proportions. Experts in the study of violent behavior theorize that the root causes in the individual stem from an underdevelopment of appropriate controls, subjugation of defenses against emotional reflexes, constitutional deficiencies that interfere with our capacity to develop control, or from physiological biochemical brain deficits (Stark 1989). Whatever the etiologies of violent behavior, destructive actions result when our critical level for tolerance is exceeded, like a vessel exploding when the inner pressure becomes too great for the skin.

Because of the worrisome reality of youth waste from runaways or suicides in our society, a better understanding of adolescent development seems fundamental. The ages from about twelve to twenty-eight may well be the most turbulent of one's life. Adolescence is defined as the period from "the onset of puberty to maturity," but "maturity" is poorly defined. Adolescence is the only time period after the first year of life that physical, psychosocial and cognitive growth accelerate at such a rapid pace. Erik Erickson, theorist and author of *The Challenge of Youth*, refers to adolescence as a time of identity crisis and psychosocial moratorium. The emotional demands on adolescents emanating from significant biological and psychosocial changes create extraordinary stress for the teenager, who is required to make that crucial transition between childhood and adulthood. During the period of physical and physiological sexual evolution, the individual is expected to attain a number of maturational goals:

a sense of sexuality; psychological separation from the family on the road to autonomy (painful for both parent and child); and a concept of self through trial and error. The formation of one's own value system versus the taught parental system or the values that society imposes is an arduous process. The requirement necessitates forming commitments to self in behavior, performance and short or long-term goals. Finally, there is the assumption of responsibility for one's own actions. For those youngsters entering adolescence who are ill-equipped, lack good self-esteem, and are without consistent values and emotional support, the foregoing tasks for resolving the transition from child to adult or for achieving an acceptable level of maturity are almost insurmountable.

RUNAWAYS

The basic difference between runaways and suicides stems from the runaway's psychological intent to survive. Adolescent runaways whose home life has become so intolerable that anything and anyplace is bound to be better than what they have tend to leap from the frying pan into the fire without foresight for the potential abuses and exploitations facing them on the streets or in cult communities. The runaway youth seeks independence and struggles for a happier life, believing naively that once away from home, he or she will gain control over life.

KATHY

When Kathy, age fourteen, "couldn't take it anymore" after three years of emotional and sexual abuse, she ran away from home. Her entire life had drastically changed after her adoptive mother was disabled in an auto accident. At the age of eleven, she had been forced to assume homemaking, nursing and baby-sitting chores for the family. Initially, with sympathetic devotion to her mother, father and younger brother, she took on these adult activities with fervor. As time demands upon her mushroomed to the exclusion of her personal development with friends and extracurricular activities, she began to feel resentment. Kathy's physiological puberty made her yearn to talk with her mother or other girls about sex. Her strictly academic time at school never permitted the opportunity for confidential chats with her peers. Then her mother returned to the hospital for surgery for several months, leaving Kathy isolated at home in farm country with only her father and brother. Her father was not one in whom she could confide. His personality (rigid, conservative and authoritarian) became overbearing. He never let up on her about keeping an impeccably neat and clean house, just as it had been before his wife became incapacitated. Not only did she substitute for her mother in homemaking and parenting but she was coerced to submit to sexual intercourse with him. He threatened to throw her out if she didn't. He rationalized that, after all, it wasn't incest since she was an adopted child; her biological mother had given her away and she was probably illegitimate, a result of her mother's promiscuous sexual behavior. Why shouldn't Kathy repay him for all those years that he had taken care of her? In the subsequent days and months of sexual abuse and his disparagement of this young girl's sense of self-value, she often thought of running away or committing suicide. Only her love for her mother and brother, combined with her fear of the outside world—the unknown—restrained her. She kept hoping that things would revert to the happy days of her childhood and thought they would as soon as her mother became well. These hopes were dashed when her mother became progressively more debilitated and her father more demanding. The night before she left, she visited her mother. They both cried, albeit for different reasons. Kathy had made her decision and said a final "good-bye" to her mother. The next morning after her father left for work and her seven-year-old brother left for school, Kathy packed her few clothes and a family picture in her nylon tote and a brown-bag lunch and other memorabilia in her schoolbag. She deliberately left her schoolbooks at home. Her purse contained $25 in savings and another $50 from the cookie jar. She boarded the school bus, but when it arrived at school, she slipped away from the other kids and, careful to avoid familiar townspeople, walked directly to the commercial bus stop.

The next bus was going to Dallas. She climbed aboard. Once in the big city, she was awestruck by the tall buildings and glamorous department stores. She had been wandering around in a daze for hours when darkness settled in, returning her to the reality that she was tired, hungry and had no place to sleep. In her desperation to escape her father and the drudgery of her existence, she had acted on an impulse to flee, just to get away, not giving a thought to what she would do when she succeeded. On the outskirts of the city, she found a fast-food place to gorge on her favorite Mexican food. Among the other teenagers there was a girl, a little older than Kathy and also carrying a tote bag. After the last of the kids had drifted off, they befriended each other. As it turned out, Kathy and her new friend had similar backgrounds: both country girls; both entrapped by abusive families; and both afraid and lonely in a strange place. They strolled around half the night and finally fell asleep on a grassy knoll hidden from the police patrol cars and the street people who might harm them. Two days later, their independence and self-protective instincts failed them. They weren't suspicious of a friendly offer from a grandmotherly type of woman who gave them home-cooked food and a place to stay in her apartment. The woman's convincing approach was that she missed her own daughters terribly and would love to have company until they could find jobs. Kathy and her friend felt secure for the first time since they had run away. How could anyone expect these naive fourteen- and fifteen-year-olds to suspect the woman of having ulterior motives? From day one, this woman drugged them by putting hallucinogens in their tea and soft drinks. Then she allowed the use of her apartment for their sexual abuse by her business partner, a pimp. Ultimately, she handed them over to him completely for a handsome finder's fee. On Kathy's first night out on the street as a prostitute, the vice squad picked her up. They learned her identity and phoned her father. He refused to take her back home and claimed that she was a "no-good kid." Kathy was remanded by the juvenile court to a home for delinquent girls. She stayed there for the next three and a half years, until she reached age eighteen.

JACK

Jack, age thirteen, typifies the case of many young boys who run away. He had been physically abused ever since he was eight years old by his alcoholic stepfather. He could never figure out what he had done to provoke the beatings, but almost on schedule and coinciding with his mother's monthly "bitchiness," the man would attack him. How Jack dreaded that unmerciful belt with the big buckle that really hurt. Before school, on the mornings after such beatings, his mother would gently treat any broken skin on his back, making sure that he wore an extra T-shirt to cover up his wounds. Eventually his seventh-grade gym teacher noticed the scars on his back during shower time. He reported to the school principal, who asked the school doctor and nurse to confirm. Suspicions of child abuse were filed with the juvenile protective agency, but it was months before the case was investigated. The beatings persisted even more vehemently. Nothing Jack did pleased his father: not more voluntary chores, not more time spent on his homework, not neater dressing, not keeping his room cleaned up. He didn't know what to do, and even hiding or fighting back as he grew bigger was unsuccessful. His last and only resort was to leave home.

On a rainy, early dismissal day from school after his most recent beating, he walked to the interstate highway and hitchhiked west with only the clothes on his back and $5 in his pocket. His mind was blank. He didn't know where he was going. He got one ride after another, mostly with truck drivers. Two days later, Jack landed in Los Angeles. His $5 already spent upon truck-stop food, he managed to get a temporary polishing job at a car wash, providing him money for food but not enough to pay for lodging. When that job ended, he and a new buddy got a ride to the beach, where they just played, swam in the ocean and slept on the sand. Stealing money, food, clothes and anything they could use became an exciting survival measure. Nevertheless, except for a few close calls with the beach patrol, this new life was the best that Jack could remember. The whole experience was too pleasurable to last—and it didn't.

During one night when they were hitchhiking up the coast toward Big Sur, they were picked up by an older man and his brother. While the boys were sleeping, the men drove them far off the highway to a remote mountain area. They were awakened and dragged out of the car and into a crudely built cabin. Subsequently, they were beaten and sexually molested daily while being chained to a bed. The boys endured a living hell for three weeks at the hands of these men before they were discarded on a highway, many hours away from the cabin. A passerby found them in a roadside ditch, bound and gagged, half-crazy, half-starved, ragged and dirty. Against the boys' protests, the Good Samaritan loaded them into his back seat and drove until he found a highway patrol police officer. It was not until the boys saw the officer's uniform that they stopped struggling and shouting obscenities. The officer transported them to the station, where they were fed, showered and given clean clothes. Later, a physician examined them. He confirmed multiple bruises and anal tears, a result of brutal sodomy. Neither Jack nor his fellow victim could or would talk coherently about their experiences. They were held under protective police custody in a halfway house for teenagers. (Adequate food and medical care would restore their young bodies in time. Much more would be required to restore their minds.)

Jack was sent to a foster care residence in his hometown while the juvenile protective agency completed their investigation of his original abuses. During the process, his mother confessed that Jack's stepfather had beaten him, causing the scars that the school doctor and nurse had identified. Because of his father's reputation in the community, no one but an experienced and knowledgeable caseworker in child abuse would have suspected him. For years he had been vice president of the local bank, a church deacon and a volunteer fund-raiser for any number of charitable organizations. The caseworker knew that child abuse exists in all sectors of society and respects no boundaries. It was a tough decision for the judge hearing the case since he had been a longtime friend of Jack's stepfather. The court had no choice but to believe the agency report and his mother's confession that Jack's father was guilty. He was sentenced to an alcohol and violence counseling program; the mother, as a silent accomplice to violence, was not charged but voluntarily sought psychotherapy. Both attended marital counseling in order to salvage their relationship. The judge was wise in taking the expert social worker's recommendations, which aimed at rehabilitative rather than punitive treatments. (Child abuse professionals should maintain the integrity of the family whenever possible.) The victim, Jack, was provided counseling for his multiple abuses. He remained in a group home setting where his treatment would be more intensive and protection from his father's residual vehemence would be secured. An additional risk from Jack's sexual abuse by male strangers was the potential for his developing AIDS, a recently identified hazard for both heterosexual and homosexual rape victims. It would be necessary for Jack to undergo HIV testing for years to come.

As a result of his mother's psychotherapy, her monthly "bitchiness" was recognized to be PMS (premenstrual tension syndrome), a treatable entity. The father was diagnosed as having a low tolerance level for criticism and denial of his libido, which had led to his displacing his frustrations and anger toward his wife upon her vulnerable son. He further revealed that because of his visibility in the community and his puritanical upbringing, an extramarital sexual affair or prostitutes were out. Beating up a child was apparently more acceptable! What does this say for his attitude toward his wife and her son? What does it say for his capacity for self-control or his ability to even temporarily cope with his anxieties? In therapy, he recalled that he had been beaten by his father. He concluded that he was following that behavioral role model when under the influence of alcohol or when shut out by his wife. His problems were so complex and deep-seated that one could predict a long-term need for psychotherapy and a less than optimistic prognosis for cure. Hopefully Jack, with earlier intervention, will be able to break the generational pattern.

SCOTT

Running away from home is not always the result of being abused or emotionally neglected. Sometimes it is to protect parents from knowing of a youth's unconventional activities for which he has shame and guilt. Such was the case with Scott. This handsome young man discovered at age fourteen that he was homosexual. By all outward appearances he was very macho, emulating his adoptive father's image. His father, a career military man, and his mother, a devoted homemaker, had been childless for the first ten years of their marriage. When the opportunity to adopt a three-month-old baby boy from a relative arose, they leaped at the chance. Scott became the focal point of their existence as they lavished him with love and attention. Growing up, Scott sensed that he was special but never suspected that he was adopted until his aunt, his actual biological mother, blurted it out in a spiteful reaction toward his parents. While the news was initially upsetting to this eleven-year-old, the bond with his dad and mom was strengthened and his gratitude toward them increased. Scott's first homosexual experience had occurred at age twelve during a weekend camping trip with his Boy Scout leader. He recalled this experience and subsequent encounters with other boys as pleasurable. Unlike most of his male friends, his newly acquired pubertal changes failed to heighten his sexual attraction for girls. Being a bigger and more well-developed boy than other fourteen-year-olds, he had no difficulty finding experienced older girls with whom to try out heterosexual intercourse. He wanted desperately to be "normal," but the truth was that his anticipated gratification fell short of what he derived from sex with males. In fact, he perceived heterosexual intercourse as more of a mechanical exercise.

The turmoil he suffered was excruciating. The realization that he was gay went contrary to every religious and societal value that he had been taught. His homosexuality would thwart his parents' dream of having a daughter-in-law and grandchildren; he was a failure. His anguish in attempting to sort out the past from the present and the future led him to behavioral changes: withdrawal from parents and peers; secretiveness and deceit; a drop in school performance; lack of appetite; insomnia; and finally drug usage. His changed deportment did not go unnoticed by his parents or others. When questioned, he was evasive and even more withdrawn. Scott thought frequently of confiding in his folks or some straight person who would accept him or help him accept himself. Because he couldn't take the risk of rejection, his torment continued incessantly, only to be abated by drugs. Suicide was entertained as one solution; another was to run away, which he did.

After a two-week escapade, he returned home, having made a decision for a compromised solution: he would continue to masquerade as a "macho" in front of his parents and peers, thus concealing his sexual preference; he would try to finish school, do as his parents wished and whenever the stresses became intolerable or when his libido became undeniable, he would run away again. Scott was convinced that his plan was the best option he could conceive in order to make life bearable and not disgrace his folks. His return home was met by ambivalence: his father was furious, his mother tearfully thankful to see him. Despite the pressure to explain why he had left, where he had gone and what he had done, Scott abstained from talking about it. With Scott's resumption of normal behavior, his father backed off on the queries and reluctantly forgave him. In fact, his father was proud of him for getting an after-school job. Little did he know that Scott's ulterior purpose was to finance his next trip. Scott left home four or five more times before he finally graduated from high school and left for good. Each time he lied to his folks about where he was going and what he was doing. In light of the popular prejudice toward homosexuals, his parents' straight, conservative ideology and the prospect of being ostracized in his suburban hometown, he was able to rationalize his deceit.

Upon high school graduation at age eighteen, Scott said good-bye and departed for parts unknown. Although he would phone on birthdays and sentimental holidays, his parents didn't see or hear from their son for four years. His return home brought a horrible shock. He was barely recognizable: pale, gaunt and prematurely aged. His parents realized that Scott was seriously ill. When he revealed to his family that he had terminal AIDS, his homosexuality seemed secondary to his imminent death. The parental reaction of disgust, shame and embarrassment that Scott had so dreaded never surfaced. They nursed him like a baby throughout each and every day of his final year. Their experience revealed important things to them. His blood relatives, including his biological mother, abandoned him; his male friends from all over the country came to comfort and to cheer him up. Henceforth, his parents, as the result of getting to know Scott's friends as decent, caring people, broadened their ideology and attitudes toward homosexuality.

SUICIDES

Other adolescents living at home, whether sober, drunk or "doped-out," feel so hopeless and helpless regarding their circumstances that suicide seems like the only escape, the one ultimate protest.

While we, parents, teachers and friends, do not always perceive the warning signals that young people send us if they are contemplating ending their lives, the signs are there. Anyone who talks about death, utters self-degrading statements, exhibits personality changes such as becoming more quiet, serious and introverted or too comically extroverted, or vice versa, is signaling. Some youngsters demonstrate habit changes in previous interests, eating, sleeping or dressing. Others become reckless and accident-prone quite suddenly. The highest risk of suicide is present in those having made prior attempts or those having a family member who had attempted or succeeded in committing suicide. On the other hand, a considerable number of youngsters who appear well adjusted and have stable, successful parents fail to give an SOS. Their final act is tunnel-visioned impulsiveness, based upon an isolated event (such as the loss of a loved one, rejection or a failure in personal performance) that overwhelms them. If youngsters felt free to pour out their emotions to parents, if parents were more sensitive to the ways their child handles loss or failure, these suicides might be preventable.

NICK

It was well past their son's midnight curfew and seventeen-year-old Nick was not home. His weary parents were growing more and more anxious since breaking a curfew for Nick was rare. The sound of his car entering the driveway would signal his safe return and allow them to go to bed with reassurance after a very long day. Rather than a car engine, the sound that interrupted their fretful silence was a piercing telephone ring. The fifty-year-old, tired, irritated father answered it, fully expecting to hear some excuse from Nick about car trouble, extended partying or whatever. The voice on the other end was a state police officer saying that Nick had been in a serious accident. He was being flown by rescue helicopter to the nearest hospital with a trauma center. The officer would not give him any details but urged his parents to get to the hospital as soon as possible. They dressed frantically and raced some sixty miles to their destination. The car was not the only thing racing during the course of their nerve-wracking drive; Mr. and Mrs. Jacob's minds were racing over so many unanswered questions, horrid visions of what might have happened to Nick in the accident and nostalgic memories of years ago when he was a little boy. Nevertheless, they both remained silent. The intermittent flashing of the oncoming headlights was almost synchronous with the flashing of their thoughts. How badly was he hurt? Would he recover without being disabled or brain damaged? Was his promising athletic career over? Was God listening to their brief pleas that their son would live and come through this okay?

Although the Jacobs had four children, Nick was the prized only son of a high school athletic director and a home economics teacher. Beginning with his first birthday gift of a tiny football, his father had groomed him throughout childhood for a career in professional sports. Nick was the epitome of all his father's dreams—a son with exquisite physical development, neuromuscular coordination and reasonably good intelligence. His eager participation and performance in Little League baseball, Mighty Mite football, class swimming competitions and youth ice hockey never disappointed his father. Nick excelled in his every athletic endeavor. Theirs was a relationship of mutual admiration since Nick also was proud of having the devoted attention of a knowledgeable coach, mentor and father. For the previous three and a half years in high school, Nick had been a star player in varsity football and baseball. As an outstanding quarterback, he had led his team to two consecutive league championships in state superbowls. Unlike many of his peers, he had little time for girls or drugs. Keeping up his grades by doing homework and studying for tests had consumed his spare time. Athletic practices and games left him exhausted, with little energy for other involvements. He fully prepared for a football scholarship from one of the Ivy League universities that had scouted him and agreed with his father that he would accept only the best offer from the school that provided him with the greatest opportunities for a good education and, at the same time, that facilitated his entry into pro-football. That chance was offered shortly after his last big game of the season, but the critical game in which Nick was to exhibit his talents before the scouts had been nothing less than a disaster. His key teammates had been sidelined by injuries or school suspensions for failing grades or drug usage; the young and inexperienced second-string did not respond to his quarterback signals. Nick himself played his absolute worst. His balloon deflated in total despair as his lifelong efforts, talent and ambitions were dashed in one miserable afternoon. His father, concealing his disappointment, consoled his son and tried to sustain his hope for the anticipated scholarship offer. On the surface, Nick appeared to let this horrible game roll off his back. He became jovial, almost comical. He dated girls almost every night, attended movies and concerts and generally acted like the usual high school senior. His parents interpreted his altered behavior as a good sign. By New Year's Eve, the time was overdue for him to have heard from any of the universities about football scholarships, a fact of which both Nick and his father were acutely aware. Mr. Jacob was planning to discuss the alternatives for the future with his multitalented son soon, but somehow, he never quite got around to it. Now it might be too late.

The Jacobs' car arrived at the hospital trauma center. It was a busy night for the doctors and nurses in emergency, so more anxious minutes were expended in waiting for the surgeon treating Nick to give them the information they sought. Nick had sustained morbid injuries to the head, neck, chest and abdominal organs. He had been delivered to the center in shock. Then he went into cardiac arrest, from which he was successfully resuscitated. He was taken to surgery in order to remove his ruptured spleen, the major bleeding source, and to repair what they could of his liver. Again he had a cardiac arrest, and this time it was intractable. Their son was dead.

Reluctantly, they viewed the barely recognizable body of their lifeless son for identification. Mrs. Jacob's sobbing and screams of pain and rage would alter nothing; Nick's father maintained extreme emotional control as he tried over and over to get some answers about the circumstances surrounding the car crash. He ran like a blind, helpless creature into the wall of bureaucratic silence. The police refused to talk until their investigation was completed. Nick's parents, like mute robots or zombies, drove the long road home. Late the next day, they learned more about the fatal accident. The Jacobs' car, occupied solely by their son, had driven straight off a mountain road. No braking marks were evident at the scene. Nick was found about 9:00 P.M., pinned inside the inverted car, located halfway down the mountainside, thus accounting for the needed helicopter rescue and transport. The coroner's autopsy findings revealed that Nick's body had sustained multiple and massive damages, any one of which could have been incompatible with life. The toxicology screen for drugs or alcohol was negative. The coroner signed the death out as accidental, perhaps showing some compassion for the family. Mr. and Mrs. Jacob knew it was a suicide and why it had happened.

As mentioned earlier, accidents are the first ranking cause of teenage death in the United States, followed by suicides. Many experts suspect that figures for suicide would be much higher if accidents were more comprehensively analyzed case by case before being labeled and categorized in a statistical pile. The age-old stigma of suicide being a disgrace and a sin against God persists in the bulk of our societal thinking. (I have a sense that the guilt surrounding the families and friends of suicidal victims make them feel that they, themselves, have failed and consequently, would prefer to deny that anyone, especially a young person, would want to take his own life.) It is an outrage that children growing up should be so fragile in self-esteem and so isolated from sensitive people in their environment that ending their lives is the exclusive solution. It is an outrage that children grow up being abused and feeling so helpless and hopeless that only death will relieve their pain.

DAMON

Damon's mother came home early from her school nursing job in order to bake and decorate for her oldest son's birthday party. Turning thirteen would be a big event and all the family—aunts, uncles and grandparents—were coming for his surprise party. As she scurried around doing all her last-minute preparations, she saw her other son, age nine, bike up the driveway. She heard him open the squeaky garage door and then heard a loud sustained screech before he came bursting into the kitchen. His utterings were incoherent as he dragged her to the garage to find Damon hanging from the rafter. Damon's color was blue to purple around the face; his body was limply dangling, telling her professional mind that he was dead. As a nurse she tried to remain calm, recalling instinctively that you never give up on a patient. She picked up the broken ladder that Damon had used. Her 5-foot, 4-inch height left her short of the level required to release the rope and lower him to the floor, where she had intended to do CPR. She raced to the phone to call 911 for help and turned to hug her equally hysterical son. She had never felt so helpless. While she waited for the EMTs to arrive she thought, "My God, where was anybody when I needed help?" Even her physician husband was unreachable; he was in an airplane flying back from a medical meeting for his son's birthday. A piercing siren heralded the arrival of the EMTs and the police. After cutting down the boy's body, the fact that he had no heart beat, no respirations and cool body temperature signified that he had been dead for a while. Someone from the coroner's office came to view the body and to investigate the circumstances of death. Although Damon's room did not contain a final note, his father's jammed revolver and his smashed computer revealed some indication of his anger and self-destructive determination.

Moments after the coroner and emergency vehicles had left with Damon's body, her husband and family members started to drive up. An anticipated joyful time turned into a premature wake. Even grief was preceded by shock and the unanswered question of why he had taken his life. No amount of going over and over the prior days and months of contact with Damon gave anyone a clue. There were no signs of changed behavior, altered attitude or signs of depression, not even a known negative event. Damon had always been a loner. Rather than spend his free time with friends, he preferred to work at his computer after school, demonstrating his prolific talent in computer literacy and mathematics. In the evenings, he enjoyed beating his father at chess. Despite his seriousness and lack of friends, he always seemed to be happy and content. Everyone knew that someday he would be a great physicist and so excused dyslexia as his one weakness. Years of tutoring had not effectively improved his reading skills. His teachers in English and social studies chronically overlooked his low grade performance in their subjects and passed him, knowing that he was an otherwise bright student.

The precipitating factors of his suicide remained unknown until several weeks after the funeral, when his guidance counselor met with his parents in their attempt to do an "emotional autopsy," one that researches the nonphysical causes leading to a death. The counselor revealed that Damon had received very low scores in the reading portions of the pre-SATs (Scholastic Aptitude Test), pulling down his top scores in math to an overall score that would deleteriously affect his acceptance into a pre-college curriculum. She had received the unfavorable report just a few days before Damon took his life. She had scheduled an appointment with him to discuss the score and his options. That date coincided with the day he died. Speculation was that Damon must have quietly received his score in the mail a day or so before then.

Damon's suicide illustrates many factors that often contribute to a teenager taking his own life. First, he was identified as a loner having no friends with whom to communicate or share in peer experiences, which are so vital to adolescent development. Second, he lacked the initiative to experiment with severing the parental umbilical cord and formulating his autonomy. Third, he possessed an adolescent sense of perfectionism based upon his mathematical skills and nurtured by his parents. His imperfection in reading abilities was ignored. Fourth, his own, his parents' and his teachers' expectations for Damon's future as a scientist were dashed because his low pre-SAT scores meant that he would not fulfill their hopes. He was a failure!

Experts in adolescent suicide could substantiate that any one of Damon's characteristics have led other teenagers to attempted or successful suicide. His profile portrayed loneliness, social isolation, perfectionism, school difficulty and high, perhaps unrealistic, parental expectations. All made him susceptible to a shame and guilt so overwhelming that he would never be able to face his parents. With tunnel vision, he chose suicide.

Eve———————————————————————————————————————

Another young life was prematurely, unnecessarily and irrationally ended at age fifteen, after two previous attempts. Eve's self-destructive behavior began two years earlier when her beloved father left home and divorced her mother. She had been so happy and doted upon as their only child. Having recently moved across the country, there were no extended family members available for support. Both Eve and her mother were emotionally devastated; each of their depressions fed off the other's. Her mother sought relief from her own pain through counseling and tranquilizers. She was oblivious to Eve's suffering. Although Eve was popular with her school friends, she could not easily talk to other eleven- and twelve-year-olds about her father's desertion, the divorce, her mother's problems and especially her own anguish. Oh, if she could only be reassured that her father still loved her and that she was not responsible for his leaving and the divorce. Mainly, she wanted desperately to talk to someone who would help her weather this first big crisis in her life. (A child of her young age and immaturity has not developed the internal or external resources of an older child or an adult.)

Mimicking her mother's example, she overdosed on a "salad" of her pills. Eve's timing was optimal for being discovered since she knew that her mother would be home soon. Her mom found her groggy and in the presence of the empty tranquilizer containers. EMTs transported Eve to the local hospital ER in time to pump out her stomach. Eve's actions resulted in her getting the help and attention she needed but couldn't ask for. This drastic act jolted her mother out of her egocentric state into an awareness of Eve's problems. Individual and mother-daughter counseling proved to be effective until Eve sustained a second emotional blow some months later.

Eve had been playing ball outdoors with her best friend, Judy, the family springer spaniel. When the ball landed across the street, Judy dashed to retrieve it and was fatally struck by a car. Another lost loved one, so soon, prompted Eve to a second suicide attempt. This time she deliberately bolted out in front of a fast-moving truck. Here again, she seemed to be using the suicide method most readily available to her by copying first her mother's and now Judy's example. Had the incident been fatal, her death would have been labeled accidental. Major surgical repairs restored her badly injured body. Intensive psychotherapy attempted to treat her reactive depression. During her prolonged recuperation, her mother—having resumed a semblance of psychological stability—lavished Eve with attention. Upon her return to school, Eve renewed her previous popularity and did well with her grades and extracurricular activities. The following year she was elected sophomore class president, a member of the high school student council and succeeded in cheerleading tryouts. Her life had assumed a new dimension with peer involvement and, on the surface, she seemed to have put her past family unhappiness behind her. Then one Saturday she saw her dad with his new young wife at a football game; unfortunately, the day after this brief incident her mother was working her hotel management job, so Eve was home alone. She cried and cried all day.

By Monday she was back at school submerging her inner feelings with a busy schedule and being more cheerful than ever with her classmates. Although she had been casually dating boys, nothing was serious until late in the spring when her football hero, a senior, asked her to the upcoming prom. Eve had been infatuated with him for months; he never seemed to "know she was alive." Her greatest fantasy was about to become reality. Euphoria prevailed over her every moment. Her girlfriends envied her. She was completely mesmerized by him to the point that when the time came, she gratefully sacrificed her virginity to please him. As the prom date grew nearer, Eve frantically searched for a gown. It had to be regal since she anticipated being crowned queen as he would be crowned king. Her choice of a dress and accessories was outlandishly expensive, far beyond her savings or her mother's budget. Happy for her daughter's achievements and as a reward for Eve's recovery, her mother sold her diamond engagement ring to buy her the gown. By 8:00 P.M., two hours after Eric was supposed to have picked her up, he hadn't shown up or called. She telephoned Eric's parents, who informed her that he had left home in his tuxedo about 5:30 P.M. It was obvious to Eve that Eric's mother was not aware that Eve was supposed to be his prom date.

Her own mother had left for work earlier after helping her dress in that gorgeous gown and taking a photo of her beautiful daughter.

Alone again! Abandoned! Deceived by her idol and lover! Robbed of her fantasy ball! What would she do? About 9:00 P.M. in utter despondence, Eve found her father's loaded handgun and shot herself in the head. Apparently, she, too, "could not take it anymore."

The deplorable fact that physically healthy young people with their whole lives ahead of them are committing suicide every year in ever-increasing numbers is a significant commentary on our society. Emotional instability, low self-esteem and mental health disorders in young people have reached unprecedented heights. Every form of child abuse and neglect has contributed to this seemingly unsurmountable problem. For the most part, youngsters who are emotionally stable, happy and living in a caring, supportive environment do not feel desperate enough to run away or take their own lives.

Until we, parents, teachers and community leaders, are ready to acknowledge the root causes that promote runaways and suicides, the rate of runaways and suicides will continue to rise. We must address our lack of sensitivity, tolerance and understanding of kids; we must make ourselves available to listen to our children and to assist them in overcoming their current crises. Such efforts may go a long way in deterring this tragic waste of young lives.

CHAPTER 8

BUREAUCRATIC INADEQUACIES

WHAT'S WRONG WITH
THE PRESENT SYSTEM?

Up to this point, the focus of this book has been upon the perpetrators and child victims of abuse/neglect. Now let us look at weaknesses within the bureaucracy. Too often, the well-intended efforts of governmental agencies and their consultants to prevent and treat neglected and abused children fall short of their goals. While the reasons are complex, some basic factors are as follows: inadequately trained investigators (such as social workers, police and so on); insufficient staff, creating case overload; inexperienced attorneys and judges in child abuse cases; poor interagency communications; erratic follow-ups; sparsity of appropriate foster care placements with trained foster parents; and biased or inexperienced psychologists. Despite the more than 150-year recognition of the problem of child abuse/neglect in the United States and the government's attempts to "prevent and treat," the present system remains in its infancy. Hopefully, with greater government appreciation of the inadequacies and increased experience on the part of trained professionals, each fault can be corrected. Among the many mishandlings of traumatized children by professionals, due to their gullibility for deceptive presentations, are false accusations, parent alienation syndrome, erroneous medical examination findings and child witness competency.

FALSE ACCUSATIONS

Child sexual molestation is a serious criminal charge. More and more it is being used as a weapon in child custody suits and by parents of children in day-care. Some attorneys, physicians, social workers and psychologists are becoming aware of the possibility of false accusations based upon inconsistent stories rendered by adults and children alike. The charge of child sexual molestation could mean a prison sentence for the accused and almost certain ruination of one's career and reputation. The investigative process alone for the purported child "victim" ensures psychological trauma; it encompasses stigmatization and frequently loss of association with a loved one.

Which child sexual abuse cases should be suspect for false accusations? "Consider the source!" my professors used to say.

(1) Accusations by a parent or child caretaker who has vengeful motivation against the accused, that is, a parent unwillingly facing divorce with the threat of joint custody or a grandparent who disapproves of a son or daughter-in-law as custodian of a grandchild.

(2) Accusations by a divorced parent who objects to joint custody or parental visitations or, in some cases, foster care parents who object to parents because they want to adopt the child themselves.

(3) Accusations by ex-spouses who object to the custody parent's life style and friends, for example, the child's father accuses the ex-wife's boyfriend of molesting the child.

(4) Cases in which the child: (a) readily volunteers his story to strangers or professionals; (b) uses explicit adult language in the description of the act; (c) is more knowledgeable about sexually related matters than is age appropriate (although with radio and television exposure and adults talking more openly about sex these days, ordinarily innocent children may appear to be sophisticated); (d) varies the story substantially in subsequent interviews; and (e) indicates a time and place for the abuse that seems unrealistic and impracticable.

(5) Biased, untrained or inexperienced professionals in child abuse who are incapable of prudently screening the accuser, the victim or the accused for spurious reporting.

PARENTAL ALIENATION SYNDROME

Parental alienation syndrome, the emotional and psychological child abuse by parents as discussed at length in Chapter Six, can be a trap for the unaware professional (lawyer, social worker or judge) in child custody litigation and allow for the custody decision to be based upon false information.

MISLEADING MEDICAL FINDINGS

Dr. Lee Coleman, a California psychiatrist studying the results of the medical examinations in children alleged to have been sexually molested, points out that "abnormal" findings in the genitoanal area are not necessarily indicative of sexual abuse (Coleman 1989). Not infrequently, the same "abnormal" findings that lawyers present as concrete evidence in court are found within the normal anatomical range of children who have not been abused. The results of a medical examination are usually taken without question by investigators, prosecuting attorneys and judges. The jury accepts the reports as convincing evidence and incontrovertible proof. The truth of the matter is that medical examinations can only objectively report findings (abnormal-normal); the causation of the findings is nonscientific speculation. The medical examiner, according to his own experience with the range of genitoanal variations in children, may subjectively decide that the findings are abnormal and "consistent with sexual abuse." Dr. Coleman stresses that without current standards for the range of normal genitoanal anatomy in children, the medical examiner may report normal variations as abnormal and set off a whole chain of fallacious evidence. In fact, some sexually abused children may have no "abnormal" physical findings at all. He further points out that laboratories may erroneously report finding an organism linked to a sexually transmitted disease in the child's specimen, supplying further falsely incriminating evidence of sexual abuse.

Dr. Coleman's recommendations for research are the following: (1) establish the range of normal genito-anal anatomy in children; and (2) obtain a second independent medical examination for the alleged victim, preferably without the history of sexual abuse. Use this information to provide an unbiased opinion and educate attorneys, judges and juries that "sexual abuse is not a diagnosis" but "an event" requiring criminal investigation rather than medical conclusion.

IS THE CHILD LEGALLY COMPETENT?

Without an adult witness to the alleged child sexual abuse, the child victim's competency as a witness becomes a vital factor in substantiating grounds for a credible accusation. It is at this root level of investigation that there is the greatest risk of false accusations. Poorly trained, inexperienced or biased professionals in psychology, sociology and law enforcement can influence the child's story right from the initial interview. It is a developmental norm for young and preadolescent children to want to please adults by saying what adults want to hear, perhaps without any bearing on the truth. Chances are that the adult accuser, usually an angry mother, has already influenced the child by the time a professional comes into the picture. Should the initial interviewer be less than completely objective or influence the child with leading questions and misinterpret what the child says or does, the whole case could be built upon falsehoods. The more the child is questioned, the more the child may build up a programmed tale, losing the ability to distinguish fact from fiction. A judge must "qualify" a child as a competent witness before his testimony can be admitted in a trial as evidence. Here again, the determination of the child's admissibility as competent is dependent upon the judge's opinion. His or her understanding of child development and child psychology, bench and lawyer experience in child abuse cases and nonemotional objectivity are prerequisites for a wise judgment. From my communication with lawyers experienced in child abuse nationwide, it appears that very few judges meet these important requirements.

DIFFICULTIES WITH FOSTER CARE PLACEMENT

Once the determination has been made that the child victim must be removed from the family and placed in a foster care home, one might sigh with relief and presume that the child has been rescued. Not so. Separation from parents, no matter how abusive, is emotionally traumatic to the child. Separation from siblings for whatever logistic reasons can be painful and anxiety provoking. Being surrounded by unfamiliar adults and children in a strange place adds to the fright of the separation experience. All too often the child has been so psychologically traumatized by past abuses that an adjustment to a new environment and people is difficult, if not impossible. Significant behavioral problems ensue with which some foster parents are unable to cope. Result: the child is moved again and again and again until he or she adapts or bonds with the foster parent. The problem lies in the lack of trained foster parents and/or careless and inappropriate placement.

Sometimes foster parents with their own biological children treat the foster child inequitably, further lowering the child's self-esteem. Other times a foster parent may abuse a child, sexually or emotionally. Thus, for the victim, the abuse may continue. After a lengthy placement in which the foster parent has bonded with the child, the substitute parents may want to adopt. This situation may promote a form of parental alienation syndrome where the child turns against his biological parents. Natural parents are put into competition with foster parents, who may resent or denigrate them, putting the foster child into an untenable position. He or she is forced to choose and the natural instinct is to love one's biological parents. Not infrequently, the child feels guilty and at fault for his parents' abusive behavior, just as many children blame themselves for their parents' divorce. In spite of past treatment, children almost always want to be with their own parents, as evidenced by the fact that large numbers of older foster children return to their parents as soon as they are emancipated from state control.

Stable grandparents, aunts and uncles of the child who are willing and able to provide a loving home are often denied the opportunity by the bureaucracy because they live out of state, complicating case management. How ironic that the sociological goal of maintaining the integrity of the family for the abused child cannot be adhered to because of bureaucratic red tape. Is inter-agency communication and cooperation so backward in this electronic age that the child can be denied the nurturing of blood relatives because of geography?

WHAT ARE THE LONG-TERM EFFECTS OF CHILD ABUSE AND NEGLECT?

The emotionally, physically or sexually abused child is affected for life with psychological scars that do not heal. The overwhelming effects of abuse during childhood, as described earlier in the book, shape the adult. Our criminal courts, jails and prisons are filled with persons whose past histories reveal that they were victims of child abuse. The mental health facilities, institutional and outpatient, are crowded with persons seeking relief from pain stemming from child abuse. Families and marriages are destroyed as a result of first- or second-generation child abuse. Dr. Frank W. Putnam, Jr., psychiatrist at the National Institute of Mental Health in Washington, DC, and a leading authority on multiple personality disorders (MPD), indicates that 97 percent of patients with MPD in his study had histories of serious childhood trauma from sexual abuse or physical abuse and a combination of both was common (Putnam 1989). He states that repetitive traumatic events over a period of years force the child to psychically disassociate in order to cope with the abusive event, achieving an altered state of consciousness. Disassociation is an adaptive process that walls off the painful memories of trauma from the general level of awareness and recall. Rather than maturing to adulthood with a sense of one identity and self, the repeatedly traumatized child, through disassociation, develops a number of separate identities and behaviors—multiple personalities. While MPD is considered a rare psychiatric disturbance, Dr. Putnam points out that victims often have been erroneously diagnosed with schizophrenia, psychotic depression or borderline personality disorder. Except for death or physical disabling, psychiatric disorders loom as the most severe long-term effect of child abuse.

CHAPTER 9

GENERATIONAL HOPE

INDIVIDUAL AND GOVERNMENTAL RESPONSIBILITIES

How far have we come as a country in eliminating child abuse and neglect since the Child Abuse Prevention and Treatment Act, also known as PL 93-247, was enacted in 1974? Statistics from the National Center on Child Abuse and Neglect in Washington indicate an alarmingly steady rise in child abuse/neglect from 1987 onward. The American Humane Association, under contract, recorded more than two million cases in 1987 (up one-half million from the previous year). In 1988, the National Center reported a 9.7 percent increase and in 1989 a 21.7 percent increase. Reflecting state increases, Massachusetts noted a rise to 17 percent in 1990—and it is still climbing in 1991. If we sit in our cozy homes and are horrified by news on television or in the papers of the latest brutal case, we must conclude that we haven't come far enough. Even one abused, sexually molested or dead child is one too many!

HISTORY OF UNITED STATES LAWS ON CHILD ABUSE

Looking at the history of child abuse and neglect in America, however, certain socially conscious, progressive states and cities have come a long way, albeit slowly. The first official legislation on cruelty to children was enacted in New York in 1875, subsequent to the Children's Aid Society in New York City in 1853. The focus then, as now, was placed upon the urban poor and destitute children who were abandoned by their parents. They were deposited in institutions or foster homes where they were provided with their basic needs for subsistence. Now with a greater awareness and sophistication, we know that child abuse and neglect is not confined to any one socioeconomic or geographic group.

The beginnings of official interest in the well-being of all children were born out of the nineteenth-century Industrial Revolution's inhumane abuses to men, women and children. This period in history saw children and married as well as unmarried women work for wages in factories under deplorable conditions. The wives of the affluent, with their nannies and housekeepers, indulged in charitable causes and social reform. These women were concerned with improving conditions in hospitals and the penal system, with the abolition of slavery, prohibition of alcohol and prostitution, organized nursing and the protection of children from cruelty. Determined to make an impact, women were on the march in 1830 to gain the right to higher education, first in women's colleges and later as coeds in the universities. Not until 1920 were women in the United States granted the right to vote.

Industrialization generated labor laws, the first of which was the Factory Act of 1922. Of the several items addressed by Congress with relevance to child abuse were the health and safety regulations regarding working conditions. Restrictions were placed upon child labor by the Fair Labor Standards Act of 1938, which stated that children were required to be a minimum age of fourteen to work in nonmanufacturing jobs after school hours; at age sixteen, children were permitted to work in jobs dealing with interstate commerce; and at eighteen, they could work in industries considered hazardous by the Labor Secretary. An indication of how well the more recent child labor laws have been implemented or enforced is the US Department of Labor report of March 1990, finding several thousand teenagers working a prohibitive number of hours per week and their work hours often extending into the late night.

Current federal labor law prohibits fourteen and fifteen year old children from working between 7 P.M. and 7 A.M. on school nights and no later than 9 P.M. on nonschool days. Operation by children under eighteen of hazardous machinery, such as slicing machines and doughnut mixers, is also prohibited. Child labor law violations have increased more than 250 percent since 1983, according to US Congressman Don J. Pease (D-Ohio). Congress has directed the Department of Labor to investigate. At least one would like to surmise that most of the youngsters are willingly working for their own money (for education, cars, clothes and recreational items) rather than being forced to earn money to help support their needy families. Some observers would say that being constructively busy is preferable to just "hanging-out" on the streets.

The first federal recognition of child abuse and neglect came in 1935 when Social Security funded public welfare services "for the protection and care of homeless, dependent and neglected children and children in danger of becoming delinquents." Although the US Congress passed the Maternity and Infant Act in 1921, most social, health and assistance reforms came after the second world war. Both the National School Lunch Act, providing a nutritional supplement for needy children, and Title V of the Social Security Act, "Aid to Families with Dependent Children"

(AFDC) made a huge improvement on child health and welfare. Federal, state and local public health programs have assisted needy parents by providing immunizations and well-child clinics, nutritional and health counseling, crippled children's clinics, prenatal care and many other essentially free services.

The next major milestone in the United States regarding awareness of child abuse and neglect occurred in 1961, when C. Henry Kempe, MD, presented the "battered child syndrome" before a broad national audience at the American Academy of Pediatrics convention. Dr. Kempe thus alerted the medical profession, professionals in social service and law, legislators and the public to the extreme physical abuse being perpetrated by parents and caretakers upon children. About 200 years before Dr. Kempe, a professor of legal medicine in France named A. Tardieu studied the autopsy reports of children and concluded that some had died as the result of nonaccidental burning or beating. Reports from London surfaced that indicated not all fractures in children were the result of commonly prevalent rickets but rather of physical abuse. In 1946, studies by J. Caffey, an American radiologist, pointed out the association between arm and leg bone abnormalities on x-rays and subdural hematomas. Until Dr. Kempe's announcement at the American Academy of Pediatrics convention, the intentional nature of traumatic injuries was not taken seriously. Dr. Kempe and colleagues demonstrated that certain combinations of traumatic injuries found on x-rays or during physical examinations of children were highly suspected of being caused by deliberate physical abuse rather than "accidental" or unintentional causes—a conclusion physicians had been led to believe by a child's history or the parents' story. By the mid-1960s, a wave of public interest had reached shore; forty-nine states had enacted laws mandating the report of any suspected cases of child abuse or neglect to public agencies and the persons reporting were offered legal immunity against suits. In 1973, a US Senate subcommittee on children and youth conducted hearing after hearing on the comprehensive dimensions of child abuse and neglect and the inadequacy of existing procedures for identification and protection. With the groundwork convincingly laid, the Child Abuse and Treatment Act became law in 1974, establishing a National Center on Child Abuse and Neglect. Its purpose was to collect information, to disseminate materials on model programs already working in some states and generally to inform the public on the subject. The act also established an Advisory Board on Child Abuse Prevention and Neglect composed of the relevant federal departments; the board's job was and is to advise the Secretary of Health, Education and Welfare regarding the coordination of federal, state, local and private agency activities in combating child abuse and neglect. The board was later expanded to public-at-large appointees and the Secretary's title was changed to Secretary of Health and Human Services.

A contract for the first National Study of the Incidence and Severity of Child Abuse and Neglect was granted in 1976 and ultimately conducted in 1979–80. Even before the incidence study was begun, the US Congress added the 1978 amendments to PL 93–247, expanding the definitions of child abuse to include sexual exploitation and the definition of neglect to include "failure to provide medical care." Shortly after the 1980 National Study was completed, the US Congress once again expanded its definitions in the 1984 amendments: a person responsible for a child's health and welfare means "any employee of a residential facility or any staff person providing out-of-home care"; regarding sexual abuse, the law specified that "anyone under 18 years old is termed a child." Previously unaddressed but now included was the medical management of disabled infants with life-threatening or nonviable conditions, more specifically, newborns with morbid congenital defects of brain, open spine or internal organs. In order to enforce this national mandate, known as the "Baby Doe" regulations, states would be denied eligibility for child abuse grant funds if they did not institute programs or procedures for treating disabled newborns in a manner prescribed by the government. ("All newborns except for certain conditions be treated with maximal life-prolonging treatment.") Because the regulations were so lengthy and complex, physicians and other professional (legal, sociological, ethical or religious) child advocates interpreted the mandate in widely diverse ways. It is my opinion that the "snitch" clause for reporting (suspected negligence in the withholding of "maximal life-prolonging treatment" to certain newborns) created a totally unnecessary havoc in the doctor–parent–patient relationship and colleagues' trust in each other's medical judgment. Of all the major advances made by the government and others to protect children from abuse and medical neglect, the Baby Doe regulations were counterproductive, divisive and, ironically, redundant. The US Supreme Court in 1986 rejected a similar version of Baby Doe regulations that had been officially announced in 1984 as an extension of the Rehabilitation Act of 1973. The basis of the Supreme Court's opinion in striking down the "extension" was the government's attempt to modify standards of medical care (a direct interference with medical judgment) and to override the parents' and physician's traditional decision making for medical management under the "best-interest standards." In spite of the court's opinion on the earlier set of Baby Doe regulations, the 1984 amendments to the Child Abuse Prevention and Treatment Act continue to be implemented. With the advances in neonatal medical technology during the late 1980s, "maximal life-prolonging treatment" can take extreme forms. The question of overtreatment arises with "Big Brother" overlooking each case. Some child protection advocates both inside and outside the government—including health care professionals—have been concerned with the potential misuse of resources (human manpower and funds); the strictest compliance to the Baby Doe regulations could potentially divert funds from other child abuse prevention programs. Does prolonging life sometimes result in prolonging suffering for the child and his parents? If so, might not this be interpreted as child abuse? Will the day come when physicians, nurses and even parents who care for those babies under legal mandate be accused of child abuse rather than medical neglect? These are some of the many questions raised by those of us concerned with the overall well-being of children and who call for a reassessment of the regulations.

In 1985, Congress, sensitized by the reports of child sexual abuse in day-care centers, appropriated $25 million to the Title XX funds for staff training. The Department of Health and Human Services was designated to develop the "Model Child Care Standards Act—Guidance to States to Prevent Child Abuse in Day-care Facilities" and distribute it to the states. The manual contains recommendations for day-care licensing standards that specifically address the following: staff training, development, supervision and evaluation; staff qualification requirements, by job classification; staff-child ratios; probation periods for new staff; employment history checks for staff; and parent visitation. More explicitly advised was an open-door policy for parent visitation without notice; information provided to parents regarding the selection of day-care facilities; the detection of signs of abuse and what action to take in suspected cases; how to implement parent involvement in the child's program; thorough personal and reference investigation of employee applicants; probationary periods with on-site checks for new child care workers; skill training for employees in the prevention, identification and reporting of abuse; and outreach community educational programs to increase awareness in the public, in parents and in children of child abuse.

Today, states vary a great deal in their day-care licensing standards and registration requirements. Those states that have followed the federal recommendations tend to offer the most protection against potential child abuse in day-care facilities.

Yes, we have come a long way; today all fifty states and the US Territories have child protective laws and programs covering all forms of child abuse and neglect (physical, sexual, emotional, medical and educational). Any person who suspects that a child under the age of eighteen is being abused or neglected can report the matter to any number of agencies whose job it is to investigate and to intercede on the child's behalf.

RESOURCES BY STATE

The states differ widely in the names of child protective agencies. The following is a list by state of the agencies to contact for information or reporting cases:

Alabama Department of Human Resources, Division of Family and Children's Services, Office of Protective Services, Montgomery, AL 36130-1801; 205-284-3850

Alaska Department of Health and Social Services, Division of Family and Youth Services, Juneau, AK 99811 Zenith 4444; 907-465-3013

Arizona Department of Economic Security Administration for Children, Youth and Families, Phoenix, AZ 95005; 602-265-0612

Arkansas Department of Human Services, Division of Children and Family Services, Little Rock, AR 72203; 800-482-5964 or 501-372-7226

California Office for Child Abuse Prevention, Department of Social Services, Sacramento, CA 95814; 916-920-1765

Colorado Department of Social Services Central Registry, Denver, CO 80218-0899; 303-893-6111

Connecticut Department of Children and Youth Services, Division of Children and Protective Services, Hartford, CT 06105; 800-842-2288 or 203-822-1918

Delaware Department of Services for Children, Youth and Families, Division of Child Protective Services, Wilmington, DE 19802; 800-292-9582

District of Columbia Department of Human Services, Commission on Social Services, Family Services Administration/Child and Family Services Division, Washington, DC 20001; 202-727-0995

Florida Child Abuse Registry, Tallahassee, FL 32301; 800-342-9152

Georgia Department of Human Resources, Division of Family and Children Services, Atlanta, GA 30309; 404-756-4200

Hawaii Department of Social Services and Housing, Public Welfare Division/Family and Children's Services, Honolulu, HI 96809; CPS Reporting Hotline; 808-832-5300

Idaho Department of Health and Welfare, Field Operations Bureau of Social Services and Child Protection, Boise, ID 83720; 208-334-5473

Illinois Department of Children and Family Services, Springfield, IL 62701; 800-25-ABUSE or 217-785-5695

Indiana Department of Public Welfare–Child Abuse and Neglect, Division of Child Welfare–Social Services, Indianapolis, IN 46225; 317-636-2255

Iowa Department of Human Services, Division of Social Services/Central Child Abuse Registry, Des Moines, IA 50319; 800-362-2178

Kansas Department of Social and Rehabilitation Services, Division of Social Services/Child Protection and Family Services, Topeka, KS 66000; 913-233-1730

Kentucky Cabinet of Human Resources, Division of Family Services/Children and Youth Services Branch, Frankfort, KY 40621; 502-564-2738

Louisiana Department of Health and Human Resources, Office of Human Development/Division of Children, Youth and Family Services, Baton Rouge, LA 70821; 504-925-4571

Maine Department of Human Resources, Child Protective Services, Augusta, ME 04333; 800-452-1999

Maryland Department of Human Resources, Social Services Administration, Baltimore, MD 71201; 410-361-2235

Massachusetts Department of Social Services, Protective Services, Boston, MA 02114; 800-792-5200

Michigan Department of Social Services, Office of Children and Youth Services/Protective Services Division, Lansing, MI 48926; 517-484-8444

Minnesota Department of Human Services, Protective Services Division, Saint Paul, MN 55155; 612-298-5655

Mississippi Department of Public Welfare, Bureau of Family and Children's Services/Protection Department, Jackson, MS 39205; 800-222-8000 or 601-372-0413

Missouri Child Abuse and Neglect Hotline, Department of Social Services/Division of Family Services, Jefferson City, MO 65103; 800-392-3738

Montana Department of Family Services, Child Protective Services, Helena, MT 59604; 406-442-2030

Nebraska Department of Social Services, Human Services Division, Lincoln, NE 68509; 800-652-1999

Nevada Department of Human Resources, Welfare Division, Carson City, NV 89710; 702-827-8686

New Hampshire Department of Health and Welfare, Division for Children and Youth Services, Concord, NH 03301-6522; 800-852-3345, Ext. 4455

New Jersey Division of Youth and Family Services, Trenton, NJ 08625; 800-792-8610

New Mexico Department of Human Services, Social Services Division, Santa Fe, NM 87504; 800-432-6217

New York State Department of Social Services, Division of Family and Children Services, State Central Register of Child Abuse and Maltreatment, Albany, NY 12243; 800-342-3720

North Carolina Department of Human Resources, Department of Social Services/Child Protective Services, Raleigh, NC 27611; 800-662-7030

North Dakota Department of Human Services, Division of Children and Family Services, Child Abuse and Neglect Program, Bismarck, ND 58505; 701-255-3203

Ohio Department of Human Services, Bureau of Children's Protective Services, Columbus, OH 43226-0423; 614-466-9824

Oklahoma Department of Human Services, Division of Children and Youth Services, Child Abuse/Neglect Section, Oklahoma City, OK 73125; 800-522-3511

Oregon Department of Human Resources, Children's Services Division/Child Protective Services, Salem, OR 97210; 503-378-6704

Pennsylvania Department of Public Welfare, Office of Children, Youth and Families, Child Line and Abuse Registry, Harrisburg, PA 17105; 800-932-0313

Rhode Island Department of Children and Their Families, Division of Child Protective Services, Providence, RI 02908; 800-RI-CHILD or 800-742-4153

South Carolina Department of Social Services, Columbia, SC 29202-1520; 803-735-7222 or 803-733-5430

South Dakota Department of Social Services, Child Protection Services, Pierre, SD 57501; 605-773-3521

Tennessee Department of Human Services, Child Protective Services, Nashville, TN 37219; 615-329-1911

Texas Department of Human Services, Protective Services for Families and Children Branch, Austin, TX 78769; 800-252-5400

Utah Department of Social Services Division of Family Services, Salt Lake City, UT 84110; 800-678-9399

Vermont Department of Social and Rehabilitative Services, Division of Social Services, Waterbury, VT 05676; 800-582-7561

Virginia, Commonwealth of Virginia Department of Social Services, Bureau of Child Protective Services, Richmond, VA 23229-8699; 800-552-7096

Washington Department of Social and Health Services, Division of Children and Family Services, Child Protective Services, Olympia, WA 98504; 800-562-5624

West Virginia Department of Human Services, Division of Social Services/Child Protective Services, Charleston, WV 25305; 800-352-6513

Wisconsin Department of Health and Social Services, Division of Community Services, Bureau for Children, Youth and Families, Madison, WI 53707; 414-289-6444

Wyoming Department of Health and Social Services, Division of Public Assistance and Social Services, Cheyenne, WY 82002; 307-328-0612

INTERAGENCY COOPERATION

Another encouraging movement in the battle against child abuse and neglect is the improvement in interagency communications and cooperation, facilitating the combined action of several departments at local, county and state level, working together on a particular case. What an improvement compared to the past in which each sovereignty stuck to its own myopic jurisdiction! Social service, mental health, public health, welfare and law enforcement are at last coming together.

The recognition that professionals in social work, law, the judiciary, education and health need to have specialized knowledge and training concerning child abuse and neglect is a vital step. Not so long ago, and even today in some places, treatment of children was considered strictly a matter of parental discretion; this was similar to the "hands off" attitude toward domestic violence, whereby women were repeatedly beaten without recourse to outside help. Today the law and self-help groups intervene and provide refuge for abused women and children in protective shelters. Still persisting in many ignorant and biased persons, lay and professional, is the opinion that a woman or a child "got what was coming to them," be it rape or a beating.

NONGOVERNMENTAL ORGANIZATIONS

Over the years more than twenty-five leading national nongovernmental organizations have shown active interest in combating the maltreatment of children. The American Humane Association (AHA) had been collecting data from local Child Protective Service agencies on the incidence and character of child abuse and neglect since 1976, some three to four years before the first government-sponsored National Study of the Incidence and Severity of Child Abuse and Neglect. The AHA's American Association for Protecting Children, in Denver, Colorado, issues professional publications and answers public inquiries regarding child protective services and child abuse/neglect (800-227-5242).

The American Academy of Pediatrics' Publications Department has professional and public educational materials and an ongoing Task Force on Child Abuse and Neglect (800-433-9016). The American Bar Association maintains a National Legal Resource Center for Child Advocacy and Protection in Washington, DC. Publications can be obtained from the National Center on

Child Abuse and Neglect, Department of Health and Human Services, through their Clearinghouse on Child Abuse and Neglect Information, P.O. Box 1182, Washington, DC 20013.

The following organizations provide educational materials or programs for the prevention of child abuse/neglect to the public, communities and professionals: the National Crime Prevention Council; the General Federation of Women's Clubs; the National Education Association; and the National Network of Runaway and Youth Services. All of the above organizations have centrally located headquarters in Washington, DC, and chapters throughout the country. For instance, the National Crime Prevention Council makes available to parents and community groups educational materials on the prevention of child abuse/neglect, instructional materials on personal safety and model prevention programs for adolescents.

Self-help groups for parents having difficulty coping with their children who have been or are close to being abused provide help nationwide under Parents Anonymous; (800-421-0353 can be called to locate the nearest of the 1200 chapters). Childhelp USA services adult and child victims of child abuse and neglect, abusers and potential abusers with comprehensive crisis counseling by mental health professionals. Their hotline is 800-4-A-CHILD. This outfit reports receiving more than sixty calls per day. A subsidiary group called the Survivors of Childhood Abuse Program trains professionals, distributes materials, refers individuals for treatment and conducts research.

As incest and other sources of child sexual abuse surface, many self-help groups, such as Survivors of Incest Anonymous, often guided by professionals who were victims themselves, are springing up everywhere. Parents United, Daughters and Sons United and Adults Molested as Children United provide group help for sexually abusive parents and victims of sexual abuse and can be contacted at 408-280-5055, P.O. Box 952, San Jose, CA.

The escalation of missing children has mounted national interest and led to the establishment of the National Center for Missing and Exploited Children (800-843-5678). It accepts reports of missing children, cases of child pornography and record sightings of missing children.

Finally, worth mentioning are the youth suicide prevention groups that locally may be known as "The Good Samaritans." They are known nationwide as the National Youth Suicide Hotline, which is located through the National Runaway Switchboard Metro-Help at 800-621-4000. The latter provides information, referral and crisis counseling to runaway and homeless youths and their families.

WHO AND WHAT TO REPORT

Since family members, friends and neighborhood persons have been the major source of reporting child abuse and neglect for the preschool child, I offer the following guidelines to laypersons suspecting the maltreatment of children:

SUSPECTED NEGLECT: (1) Repeated poor hygiene and inappropriate clothing; (2) constant hunger (stealing or begging for food); (3) chronic fatigue; (4) repeated absence of supervision by the parent for unsafe activities; and (5) untreated or infected wounds, physical or medical problems.

SUSPECTED PHYSICAL ABUSE: (1) Any bruises, cuts or injury marks that are unlikely to be self-inflicted; (2) more than the average number of bruises, cuts or other injuries (a swollen limb may be the sign of a fracture in a two-year-old or younger child); (3) marks around the face and neck (black eyes, cut lip, chipped teeth, swollen nose, ears and so on); (4) welts on the back, buttocks, chest, abdomen or limbs; and (5) burns anywhere.

BEHAVIORAL SIGNS OF ABUSE: (1) Frightened of parents; (2) frightened of being touched or of any physical contact with adults; and (3) overly aggressive or withdrawn with persons familiar to them.

Suspected Sexual Abuse: (1) Combinations of the following: newly acquired difficulty in gait or sitting, blood-stained underpants, itching or pain in the genital area; (2) unexpected age-related knowledge of sexual activity; (3) any credible report of being physically or sexually abused by a parent, older child or adult. (Reports will often come secondhand through your own child from their abused friend.)

While the majority of child abuse and neglect victims come from dysfunctional parents who belittle or denigrate the child, show little concern for the child's welfare and might yell or hit the child in public, the image-correct parent who is abusive behind closed doors is probably more dangerous. Abuse and neglect recognizes no human boundaries and the more sophisticated among us tend to be the more successful in covering up their cruel behavior. Remember that physical and sexual abuse is episodic whereas neglect is chronic.

What Is the Personal Risk to You for Reporting Child Abuse or Neglect?

Both lay and professional persons who report their suspicions of child abuse/neglect have civil and criminal immunity in all fifty states, Washington, DC, Guam, Puerto Rico, the Virgin Islands and American Samoa. Depending upon your state laws, you could be penalized for *failing* to report. For the most part, professionals in medicine, nursing, psychology, education, law enforcement, social services, child care and administrators involved with children are mandated to report under penalty. It is advisable to check the laws in your own state. In any case, anyone suspecting child abuse/neglect may save a life or prevent future trauma by merely making a phone call to your child protective agency.

HOW TO REPORT AND POSSIBLE CONSEQUENCES

Take the example of Mrs. Bolger, a widowed, middle-aged housewife and grandmother living in Massachusetts in a dense residential section of Boston, who had repeatedly observed a four-year-old neighbor child scampering about the sidewalk and streets without supervision and consistently wearing clothes inappropriate to the climatic season. On her way back from the grocery store, the little boy would often come up and ask her for food from her bulging market bags. Usually she gave him some chips or cookies or whatever was convenient. She already suspected that he was neglected but on the day she saw him with a black eye and a cut lip, she knew that she had to report his condition to somebody.

The following is a step-by-step walk-through for reporting suspected child abuse/neglect in Massachusetts. (This should be used as a general guide. Contact the appropriate child protective agency in your state for specific variances.)

(1) Prepare yourself with the name, address, approximate age of the child and the nature of the injury or signs of neglect.

(2) Call the nearest office of the Department of Social Services (DSS) Child Protective Agency during weekdays or the 800 state hotline number after hours, on weekends and on holidays.

(3) Your report of suspected child abuse/neglect will be received and a determination made as to whether the situation is an emergency. A professional screening unit with DSS will interview you by telephone. Unless you are a professional or a person mandated by law to report child abuse, it is likely that your involvement will be over after you report your suspicions. The agency respects the confidentiality of its sources so that unless you identify yourself to other persons, no one need know and you may remain anonymous.

(4) If the situation is determined an emergency because the child appears to be in immediate danger, the agency's investigating caseworker must complete the investigation within twenty-four hours. An on-site visit to the child's residence will be made. The child, other children, the caretakers and the suspected abuser will be questioned. Should the questioning give the caseworker the impression that persons around the child are out of control because of drugs or alcohol, the police will accompany the caseworker to the home for everybody's safety. If the child appears to be in immediate danger, the child will be removed from the home by presumptive custody until the court can rule and be placed temporarily in a foster home. After a complete investigation is made, the agency will present the case to the court for ultimate disposition. Only in cases of severe physical abuse or sexual molestation is a referral made to the district attorney's office for potential criminal prosecution. The district Attorney will have the discretion as to whether criminal charges will be brought against the child's alleged abuser.

(5) Most of the time the situation will be determined not to be an emergency, in which case a report must be investigated within ten calendar days. Either a letter is sent to the child's caretaker regarding the complaint or telephone contact is made to set up an appointment for a home visit to assess the situation and to determine what is needed to remedy the problem. More often than not, a supportive service, such as day-care, homemaker services, medical attention or counseling for the caretaker, will alleviate the problem. The caseworker, through networking, is able to make the necessary arrangements. Every attempt is made to maintain the integrity of the family and keep children with their parents. Follow-up for ongoing reassessment is part of the casework.

Somewhat encouraging in the cause of interceding in child abuse/neglect is increased public awareness, as evidenced by increased reporting. In the small state of Massachusetts, the Child Abuse and Neglect unit of DSS had 71,713 cases reported in 1989; in June 1990, the 82,831 reported cases reflected a 17 percent increase. Very disheartening is that some 900 children were in foster homes and from January to May 1990, 49 children died from child abuse or neglect.

Increased unemployment will create an increase in child abuse and neglect. Budget constraints and cutbacks will surely mean that investigations will fall behind demand, which in turn will result in uninterrupted maltreatments of children. Perhaps, other than for reasons of conscience, the latter is an even greater incentive to become involved as watchdog, reporter or volunteer to public and private organizations that aim to prevent child abuse and neglect.

IN CONCLUSION

What we have seen through this book's many case histories are children being abused without significant provocation. Is this really the situation? I think not. Impulsive, one-time abuse is perpetrated on little kids such as Eddie, age three, who defecated and played with his feces on his mother's new carpeting, and Joshua, age four, who deliberately urinated on his parents' bed and provoked a disciplinary action on their part. Did these children deserve brutal beatings? The line between discipline and abusive punishment for children overlaps in the mind of caretakers and their interpretation of the act committed.

There is too large a proportion of society that accepts violence and sexual exploitation as inevitable. These people have often forgotten their own past hurtful experiences. Although they may have completely repressed their own abuse, it causes them to act out reflexively. The tendencies toward abusing or exploiting children, in whatever manner, are deeply rooted in our own early childhood experiences. Such traits can be passed from generation to generation.

Persistent child physical abusers must be identified, intercepted and treated. Take the case of Diane, the eight-year-old whose father and mother viciously beat her without any particular provocation except that she was accessible to them to vent their anger; or Phillip, whose parents almost crippled him for life by caning his feet. Children with handicapping conditions such as mental retardation or emotional disturbances are highly vulnerable to abuse and neglect because of the extraordinary demands that their mere existence makes upon their caretakers. Six-year-old handicapped Joey, whose feet and buttocks were burned by cigarette butts, was the victim of a sadistic person whose deliberate acts went beyond the impulse for physical punishment and became sheer torture for Joey.

Like the handicapped, unwanted children are at a very high risk for maltreatment and even homicide. Perhaps two-year-old Amy, who was nearly drowned in the bathtub and had sustained multiple nonaccidental bruises to her body, is a good example of a basically unwanted child. In light of all we knew about Amy from when she was first hospitalized for "failure to thrive," then her near-death from drowning, to the fact that she was later reported as a "missing child," we have to conclude that she was a victim of abuse and neglect for all of her short life. Babies who cry incessantly, and there are many who do so without known cause, frustrate the most stable of parents. The unwanted child provokes an impulsive overreaction from the emotionally unstable caretaker or one who is uninhibited due to alcohol or drug affects. This was the situation with five-month-old Marty, who died in the hospital ER from a skull fracture after being thrown to the floor.

Whether or not violence inflicted upon children is impulsive or chronic, it must be stopped at its root in the family by each and every bystander immediately—not hours, days or months later by some governmental agency. If Diane's neighbor had been able to muster the fortitude to go next door and inquire about the screams she heard, Diane might have been spared future beatings until the authorities could intercede. I am all in favor of privacy in the home, but when it's apparent that things are out of control, it's not the time to "mind your own business."

Adults ranging in age from thirty to sixty years old are now revealing their experiences with early childhood sexual abuse almost daily in mental health professionals' offices, self-help groups and on national radio and television talk shows. Some victims have been troubled all of their lives. Some attempted suicide in adolescence; others turned to prostitution. Some victims became homosexual; others, especially in earlier times, sought refuge in the church by pursuing a celibate existence. Rarely does a molested child survive unscathed from the experience. Gail, who was sexually molested from ages eleven to fourteen by her father, became promiscuous, not because she liked sex but because of low self-esteem. While she was fortunate enough to achieve a normal marital relationship, she was left with the consequences of her early experiences: sexually transmitted pelvic inflammatory disease caused scarring of her fallopian tubes, preventing her from conceiving a child. For many persons sexually abused as children, a loving sexual relationship in marriage is not possible. The sexual act has become imprinted as nonpleasurable, mechanical and even frightening—a method used to overpower and control not just the body but the mind. Whether we believe that sexual abuse is more prevalent in today's society or that it is just out of the closet, it is ruining lives.

In addition to those lives devastated by incest, sexual abuse and molestation, the innocently accused should not be overlooked. In a marital relationship gone sour, it is usually the father who may be fallaciously alleged to have molested his own beloved daughter or son. Examples of such false accusations are the case histories of Tanya and Jakina: Tanya's mother, because of persistent jealously and a custody battle, falsely accused her father of sexual molestation. In the process, she ruined her own credibility with family, friends and professional associations, caused irreparable damage to her former husband's career and unnecessarily subjected five-year-old Tanya to psychological examinations. Jakina's mother, frustrated by her husband's lack of interest in sex with her and jealous of the attention paid to her daughter, falsely accused the stepfather. The reason for his marital inattention was a high blood pressure medication that made him impotent. His impotence was easily corrected by a change in drug prescription; the reestablishment of his self-image as a good stepfather and husband was not as dramatic or rapid.

Society has apparently reached a point where a father who bathes, diapers and comforts a child at bedtime or even holds him on his lap runs the risk of becoming suspected of some sort of sexually motivated act during a future marital dispute.

One's constitutional rights regarding the issue of child pornography is currently before the US Supreme Court. Many of us have become very sensitive to the upsurge in child pornography as big business and an extreme form of child sexual exploitation. Those adults who seek sexual pleasure in seeing naked boys and girls frolicking around exhibiting or playing with each others genitals are not only taking advantage of a normal inquisitive stage of child development but as voyeurs are psychologically disturbed people. Their perception of innocent child play is cast in adult sexual fantasy. If the child is young enough and is not coerced, the photography itself may not affect him or her in years to come. A more serious problem arises when older children are forced to expose their naked bodies or engage in sexual acts with each other or with adults. The resulting harm may be significant as they are introduced to drug usage, prostitution and slavery.

The newest phenomenon of recognizable child abuse/neglect occurs prior to the child's birth in the prenatal period. Prenatal child abuse/neglect should be one of the easiest to prevent, having only one individual—the pregnant woman—to deal with, yet it has become among the most difficult. The mother's habits, health and life-style, upon which the developing baby is totally dependent, are impossible to control. All the amazing medical sophistication today in prenatal care (detection, treatment or prevention of birth defects, Rh-blood incompatibilities, anemia, nutritional deficiencies, venereal diseases, rubella, herpes and so on) is able to do little in reducing overall neonatal morbidity and mortality. Little Ricardo might have avoided being born with herpes encephalitis and later having developmental disabilities had his mother undergone prenatal examinations.

Pregnant girls and women persist in behavioral habits that are deleterious to their developing fetus and fail to obtain early and periodic prenatal care. The drug usage epidemic among young mothers-to-be is taking its toll on the current newborn population. In 1989, 300,000 babies in the United States were born with crack addiction; 11 percent of all babies are born with drugs in their system. Drug screening of women in a medium-size northeastern city admitted to a city hospital in labor revealed that four out of five had taken illegal drugs or alcohol within forty-eight hours of delivery. In May 1990, the national media reported that more than two million persons are cocaine addicts and that the majority of cocaine users are white. Let's assume that nearly half of these persons are females of reproductive age. No matter how one juggles the population figures, we cannot say that drug addiction in mothers is confined to poor, disadvantaged, single black women, as was the case thirty years ago. The problem bridges all socioeconomic and educational levels, race and skin color, and encompasses professional to unskilled persons. Not only are the babies of drug-addicted mothers at high risk for congenital defects, HIV and possible mental retardation, they are frequently unwanted, without an identifiable father. Ahab, who was born drug-addicted and had to suffer through withdrawal and abandonment by his mother, was one of the more fortunate babies with similar backgrounds. Newborns with AIDS, such as Megan, Jesse and Jose, were the least fortunate. Without effective treatment, AIDS babies are doomed to live out their short lives in sickness and isolation from family.

The impact to society and the newborn infant with fetal alcohol syndrome is horrendous. Fetal alcohol syndrome is the leading cause of nongenetic mental retardation. Almost any baby or child with congenital defects of heart, liver or kidneys can be salvaged these days with optimal organ transplant resources. Those who are brain-damaged as a result of maternal alcohol ingestion or drug usage are incurable.

One of the deepest humanitarian concerns our society faces today is the high rate of teenage pregnancy with inevitable consequences to the child, mother and subsequent generations. With neither intention nor foresight, the government's social reform in providing aid to families with dependent children has indirectly encouraged some young girls to have babies and live independently without supervision from their families. In essence, it has encouraged child abuse and neglect, particularly educational neglect, for the teenage mother. The temporary solution is to provide support services to mother and child: early-child day-care and education or skill training for the adolescent mother. This phenomenon was demonstrated in the case of Ginger, age thirteen years, a third-generation welfare recipient who was rebelling against her single alcoholic mother. She wanted her own place without rules. In her isolation from family and adult supervision, her baby was highly vulnerable to abuse and neglect by either Ginger or one of her boyfriends. Juli, pregnant at age fourteen, had family support until her mother developed cancer; she was compelled to quit school in order to take care of her baby with cerebral palsy. Let's not forget Melissa, whose adolescent drive to be accepted by her peers led her to bulimia, drugs and sex, resulting in an unwanted pregnancy. Parental understanding and support provided her with drug rehabilitation, psychological counseling and good prenatal care. The outcome was favorable as the baby was healthy and adoptable, allowing Melissa to return to school in pursuit of an education.

An optimistic sign for children of faith or spiritual healers who deny their sons or daughters access to medical care is that the courts throughout our land are currently hearing cases of manslaughter and medical neglect. Ultimately, the US Supreme Court will be asked to deliberate on the constitutional issue of freedom of religion verses a child's right to health and survival. More and more, our society is confronted with ethical and legal questions on the individual rights of adults who adopt habits such as smoking nicotine, who drive while intoxicated and who engage in drug-altered behavior that jeopardizes or infringes upon the rights of others. The law has already imposed sanctions and penalties upon smoking in airplanes, public buildings, restaurants and the work-place. The pregnant woman who exposes her unborn child to hazardous agents endangers the lifelong existence of a future citizen. (To the "right to life" advocates, as a physician who has taken care of the institutionalized multihandicapped, I would humbly submit that there are worse fates than death.)

It is indeed ironic that with all of the good done through the ages by the leading Christian churches (such as establishing hospitals and sponsoring medical and social missionaries in an attempt to improve human life throughout the world), spin-off messianic cults with counterculture agendas, inhumane rituals and sacrifices grow and thrive in the late twentieth century. Greed and power, cruelty and subjugation are not unknown in the history of the major religions, but persons with a rational humanitarian sense and free will usually choose the good features of the church and tend to sidestep the bad. Not so for naive young people who are mesmerized by cults and then reduced to utter dependency. Tragically, the very goals sought by youngsters in their late teens and early twenties (independence from parents and authority figures, attainment of an existence devoid of rules and regulations and the finding of one's self in a meaningful life-style) are drastically compromised. Some of our missing youth are undoubtedly being hidden in anonymity by cults, many of whom require an absolute transfer from biological family to cult "family." The premeditated techniques for conversion and sustainment of young minds to cult doctrines constitute one of the highest degrees of psychological abuse.

The previously described cases of emotional abuse tell me in retrospect that more personal self-control and sensitivity to our children's needs might have spared them psychological injury. Recall the situation of Mario, Jr., age five, and his sister, Rosa, age three, whose drunken father repeatedly locked Mario in a dark closet and tied Rosa to her high chair when they misbehaved. Compared to the beatings that Mario's father gave him, he considered his discipline an improvement. Maybe it was, but Mario, Jr., developed morbid phobias of the dark and closed doors that plagued him until, as an adult, he got psychotherapy. Rosa was tactile defensive all her life. Other children suffer as a result of their parents' unhappiness; Paul's mother was frustrated with her mostly absentee and suspectedly unfaithful husband and she displaced her anger by belittling, berating and scapegoating her son. Until Paul's mother resolved her problems in psychotherapy, through divorce and a new relationship, Paul was the helpless victim.

Children with persistent bed-wetting or fecal soiling beyond the expected age for voluntary control may be reacting subconsciously to some earlier psychological trauma, which is only aggravated by harmful parental responses. The stigma to the child endures into adulthood, as revealed by a young man of twenty-five I knew as a patient years ago. Despite his success, apparent well-adjustment and happiness with his impending marriage, he said, "You know, Dr. M., I was a bed-wetter until I was thirteen...and my parents tried everything." Eloise, reacting to her mother's illness, Grandma's strict training methods and later ridicule by her parents, was a bed-wetter until age seventeen, when she left home. Obnoxious habits such as bed-wetting or fecal soiling may be interpreted as a form of rebellion and revenge toward the parent. Ironically, such habits boomerang onto the child when he or she continues to incur negative parental responses and social restrictions.

Manipulation of children as described in the parental alienation syndrome and seen in acrimonious divorce and custody suits is one more deliberately cruel form of child abuse. My recommendation here is for the alienated spouse's family, friends, attorneys and therapists to identify the problem and offer realistic support to the child and the maligned spouse. An awareness of the problem by the disturbed spouse's professional contacts could be enough to abort the process and save the child the psychological trauma of rejecting a parent.

The escalation in teenage suicide is a horrid reflection on the mental health of our society. When our young people are so poorly equipped to cope with painful experiences (losses and failures), so emotionally, physically or sexually abused, or so hopelessly desperate as to resort to ending their lives, it says that we, as parents or caretakers, are doing something very wrong. Whether we abuse and neglect our children unconsciously or deliberately, the end result to the child is the same.

Had fourteen-year-old Kathy not been sexually and emotionally abused by her adoptive father and had she not been socially isolated from her mother, friends and neighbors, she might not have been compelled to run away, only to be further exploited. Even if her father had been able to assume some conscious responsibility for her, rather than dumping her into state care, she might have avoided ending up in an institution for delinquents. Jack, through no fault of his own, was a similar victim who was physically abused at home and later raped by strangers, except in his case, the child protective and treatment system stepped in.

There *is* hope for helping current and future generations. Thousands of laypersons and professionals are devoted to the prevention and treatment of child abuse/neglect and resources are growing every day. These caring individuals need volunteers, funds and, most of all, the ongoing support of the public. Awareness of the availability and accessibility of child help organizations must be heightened for full utilization. School, church, sports and parents' groups should be encouraged to sponsor programs on child abuse/neglect. If some of the children in this book had known where to get help, the course of their lives might have been different.

Aside from the complex moral, ethical, cultural and socio-economic factors, the real hope of preventing child abuse and neglect in this generation lies, here and now, on individual action. The time is past for gasping in shock, sighing or wringing our hands. Every man, woman and older child must first take the responsibility for his or her own behavior and second, assume responsibility for the less responsible. Present-day victims such as Ryan White, a hemophiliac boy who recently died of AIDS from a blood transfusion and little Adam Walsh, whose father initiated a crusade for missing children after Adam was found brutally murdered, have demonstrated the power of individual action. Laws are in place. Funding is available for child abuse prevention and treatment, but the responsibility remains with the *individual*. No truth is more applicable to the scourges of today's society—violence, drugs, rape, AIDS—than "the enemy is within."

As long as women are being raped or beaten, children are being abused and all kinds of senseless violent crimes against the defenseless are being committed, I will be reminded of Robert Frost's poem, "Stopping by the Woods on a Snowy Evening":

> *The woods are lovely, dark, and deep,*
> *But I have promises to keep,*
> *And miles to go before I sleep,*
> *And miles to go before I sleep.*

BIBLIOGRAPHY

Adams, Caren, et al. 1981. *No More Secrets*. San Luis Obispo, CA: Impact Publishers.

Appel, Willa. 1983. *Cults in America: Programmed for Paradise*. New York: Holt, Rhinehart & Winston.

Armstrong, Louise. 1984. *The Home Front (Notes from the Family War Zone)*. New York: McGraw.

Benton, William, et al., eds. 1975. *Encyclopedia Britannica, XVth Ed*. Chicago: Encyclopedia Britannica.

Blanche, S., et al. 1989. Prospective Study of Infants Born to Women Seropositive for Human Immunodeficiency Virus Type 1. *New England Journal of Medicine* 320 (no. 25):1643.

Brookside Hospital. 1989. *Network News*. Vol. 2, no. 1:1, 2, 3, 7. Nashua, NH: Kid Net.

_____. 1990. School Phobias. *Grand Rounds Review*: 4 (March): 6.

Cashell, et, al. 1989. Radiologic Contributions to the Investigation of Fatal Infant Abuse. *New England Journal of Medicine* 321 (no. 23):1045.

Chase, Naomi Feigelson. 1975. *A Child is Being Beaten: Violence Against Children, an American Tragedy.* New York: Holt, Rinehart & Winston.

Chasnoff, I. J., et al. 1990. Prevalence of Illicit-Drugs or Alcohol Use during Pregnancy and Discrepancies in Mandatory Reporting in Pinellas County, Florida. *New England Journal of Medicine* 322(no. 17):1202.

Coleman, Lee. 1989. Medical Examinations for Sexual Abuse: Have We Been Misled? *The Champion.* (Nov.):5–21.

Collins, Marylin C. 1977. *Child Abuse: A Study in Child Abuse in Self-Help Group Therapy.* Littleton, MA: Pub. Sciences Group.

Combrinck-Graham, Lee. 1989. Systemic Approach to Understanding Violence in Children and Adolescents. *Grand Rounds Review* 3 (no. 5):1–3.

Ebon, Martin. 1976. *The Satan Trap: Dangers of the Occult.* Garden City, NJ: Doubleday.

Edwards, Christopher. 1979. *Crazy for God.* Englewood Cliffs, NJ: Prentice-Hall.

Farberon, Morman. 1980. *Many Faces of Suicide (Indirect Self Destructive Behaviors).* New York: McGraw-Hill.

First Church of Christ Scientist. 1989. *Freedom and Responsibility, Christian Science Healing for Children.* Boston, MA: First Church of Christ Scientist.

Fontana, Vincent. 1973. *Somewhere a Child Is Crying.* New York: Macmillan.

Freeman, J. M., et al. 1988. "Baby Doe" Regulations. *New England Journal of Medicine* 319(no. 11, Sept. 15):726.

Gardner, Richard A. 1986. Psychiatric Disturbance Produced in Children by Prolonged Litigation. *Child Custody Litigation: A*

Guide for Parents and Mental Health Professionals. Cresskill, NJ: Creative Therapeutic Press.

Gellert, G. A., et al. 1989. HIV infection and Child Abuse. *New England Journal of Medicine* 321(no. 10, Sept. 7):685.

Gordon, Linda. 1988. *Heroes of their Own Lives (The Politics and History of Family Violence)*. New York: Viking Penguin.

Gross, Beatrice, et al. 1977. *The Children's Rights Movement (Overcoming the Oppression of Young People)*. Garden City, NJ: Anchor Press/Doubleday.

Guyer, B., et al. 1989. Intentional Injuries among Children and Adolescents in Massachusetts. *New England Journal of Medicine*. 321(no. 23, Dec. 7):1584

Hafen, Brent Q., and Kathryn J. Frandsen. 1986. *Youth Suicide. IInd Ed.* Evergreen, CO: Cordillera Press.

Hawkins, Paula. 1986. *Children at Risk (My Fight Against Child Abuse)*. Bethesda: Adler & Adler.

Hendin, Herbert. 1982. *Suicide in America*. New York: Norton.

Hoff, R., et al. 1988. Seroprevalence of Human Immunodeficiency Virus among Childbearing Women: Estimation by Testing Samples of Blood from Newborns. *New England Journal of Medicine* 318(no. 9, March 3):525

Hollander, Nancy, et al. 1989. The Incompetent Child Witness. *The Champion* 13-16 (Nov.)

Kane, Geoffrey. 1989. Recovery and Reintegration. *Grands Rounds Review* 3(no. 4):1-2.

Katz, S. L., et al. 1989. Human Immunodeficiency Virus Infection of Newborns. *New England Journal of Medicine* 320(no. 25, June 22):1687

Kempe, Ruth S., et al. 1978. *Child Abuse.* Cambridge, MA: Harvard University Press.

Kleinman, Paul K., et al. 1989. Radiologic Contributions to the Investigations and Prosecutions of Cases of Fatal Infant Abuse. *New England Journal of Medicine* 320(no. 8, Feb. 23):507.

Krugman, Richard D. 1989. Advances and Retreats in the Protection of Children. *New England Journal of Medicine.* 320(no. 8, Feb. 23):531.

Landau, Elaine. 1984. *Child Abuse: An American Epidemic.* New York: J. Messner.

Langone, John. 1986. *Dead End: A Book About Suicide.* Boston: Little, Brown.

Larsen, Egon. 1971. *Strange Sects and Cults.* New York: Hart Publishing.

Ledger, W. J., et al. 1988. Neonatal Herpes Simplex Infection. *New England Journal of Medicine* 319(no. 13, Sept. 29):872.

Little, R. E., et al. 1989. Maternal Alcohol Use During Breast-Feeding and Infant Mental and Motor Development at One Year. *New England Journal of Medicine* 321(no. 7, Aug. 17):425

Maharay, Davan. 1989. Abused Babies Overflowing Shelter in Orange County. *Los Angeles Times.* (Dec. 18).

Mashek, John W., et al. 1990. Probers Cite 7,000 Child Labor Abusers. *Boston Globe.* (March 16)

Massachusetts Department of Public Health. 1990. *AIDS—Guidelines for Physicians & Health Care Providers on HIV Counseling, Testing and Early Treatment.* (Feb.): Boston, MA.

Maynard, E. C., et al. 1989. HIV Infection in Pregnant Women in Rhode Island, 1985–1988. *New England Journal of Medicine* 320(no. 24, June 15):1626.

McKusick, Victor A. 1986. *Mendelian Inheritance in Man.* Baltimore: Johns Hopkins University Press.

Melville, Keith. 1972. *Communes in the Counterculture.* New York: Morrow.

Moffet, Penelope. 1989. Parent Help. *Los Angeles Times.* (July 11).

Monfalcone, Wesley. 1980. *Coping with Abuse in the Family.* Philadelphia: Westminster Press.

Monookin, Robert H., et al. 1985. *In the Interest of Children (Advocacy Law Reform and Police Policy).* New York: Freeman & Company.

National Center for Missing and Exploited Children—with the FBI. 1987. *Child Molesters: A Behavioral Analysis (For Law-Enforcement Officers Investigating Cases of Child Sexual Exploitation).* 2d ed. (April).

Nelson. 1983. *Textbook of Pediatrics.* Philadelphia, PA: WB Saunders.

O'Leary, Kevin. 1989. Child-Abuse Reports Continue Steady Rise. *Los Angeles Times.* (July 11).

Polansky, Norman A., et al. 1981. *Damaged Parents (An Anatomy of Child Neglect).* Chicago: University of Chicago Press.

Putnam, Frederick W., Jr. 1989. *The Diagnosis and Treatment of Multiple Personality Disorders.* New York: Guilford Press.

_____. 1990. Multiple Personality Disorder. *Grand Rounds Review* 4(no. 2):1–5.

Quinn, T. C., et al. 1989. AIDS in the Americas: An Emerging Public Health Crisis. *New England Journal of Medicine* 320 (no. 15, April 13):1005.

Raichlen, Steven. 1989. Healing a Secret (Incest). *The Boston Globe* (Sept. 24).

Rivara, F. P., et al: 1989. *Pediatrics.* 84(December):1011-1016.

Sargent, John. 1989. Adolescent Suicide. *Grand Rounds Review* (no. 3):1-3.

Sloan, Irving J. 1983. Child Abuse: Governing Law and Legislation. *Legal Almanac Series* (no. 79). New York: Oceana Publications.

Stark, Amy. 1989. Child's Rights Need Respect Too. *Los Angeles Times* (August 12).

Tanner, M. A., et al. 1988. Impact of Televised Movies about Suicide. *New England Journal of Medicine* 318(no. 11, March 17):707.

United States Department of Health and Human Services. 1984. *Perspectives on Child Maltreatment in Mid'80s.* Washington, DC: National Center on Child Abuse and Neglect.

_____. 1986. *Child Sexual Abuse Prevention: Tips to Parents.* Washington, DC: National Center on Child Abuse and Neglect.

_____. 1986. *Report to Congress: Joining Together to Fight Child Abuse.* Washington, DC: National Center on Child Abuse and Neglect.

_____. 1988. *Study Findings: Study of National Incidence and Prevalence of Child Abuse and Neglect.* Washington, DC: National Center on Child Abuse and Neglect.

_____. 1989. *Child Abuse and Neglect: A Shared Community Concern*. Washington, DC: National Center on Child Abuse and Neglect.

Vachss, Andrew. 1989. How We Can Fight Child Abuse. *Parade Magazine* (Aug. 20).

_____. 1990. Today's Abused Child Could be Tomorrow's Predator. *Parade Magazine* (June 3).

Zuckerman, B. 1990. Effects of Maternal Marijuana and Cocaine Use on Fetal Growth. *New England Journal of Medicine* 320 (no. 17, April 26):762.

INDEX